To my long-time friends –
Bob & Marilyn –

with love

Evelyn Carrie Birkby

MW00469605

Witching
for
William

by

Evelyn Corrie Birkby

Honey Hill Books

HONEY HILL
B·O·O·K·S

Published by Honey Hill Books
www.honeyhillbooks.com

Copyright © 2008 by
Evelyn Corrie Birkby

Design by Amy Smith
www.amysmithcreations.com

All rights reserved. No part of this book may be reproduced in any form or by any means without the prior written consent of the Publisher, excepting brief quotes used in reviews.

Unless otherwise noted, all photographs are from the author's collection.

Publisher's Cataloging-In-Publication Data

Birkby, Evelyn.

   Witching for William / by Evelyn Corrie Birkby.

        p. : ill., maps, geneal. table ; cm.

   Includes bibliographical references and indexes.
   ISBN: 978-0-9615636-2-2

1. Corrie, William, 1766-1835--Family. 2. Corrie family.
3. Lawrence County (Ill.)--Genealogy. 4. Illinois--Genealogy.
5. Scotland--Genealogy. 6. Genealogy. 7. Cookery, Scottish. I. Title.

CS71.C796 2008
929.2   2007939725

Printed in the United States of America
Library of Congress Control Number: 2007939725

ISBN: 978-0-9615636-2-2

Cover photograph - Evelyn Corrie Birkby at Borgue Cemetery, Scotland.
(photograph from Evelyn Corrie Birkby Collection)

Corrie family crest and motto
"Vigilant and Audacious"

Dedicated to my children:
Dulcie Jean Birkby
Robert Corrie Birkby
Jeffrey Lawrence Birkby
Craig Steven Birkby

And to my grandchildren:
Nicholas Craig Birkby
Amanda Mae Birkby

Who all carry the blood of our
ancestor William Corrie in their veins.

Contents

Foreword

On a hot August day, my distant cousin Dallas Krumm and I were witching for William. Dallas had cut a clothes hanger in half and bent each section of wire into an "L" shape. As he walked slowly over the black soil and dry grasses of the eastern Illinois farm field, he held the wires by their shorter lengths in his sturdy, work-worn hands, and pointed the longer portions of the wires in the direction his slow steps were taking him.

"If we come close to William's grave, the wires will pull toward one another and cross," he explained. "Anything that disturbs the Earth's magnetic field is a candidate for discovery by witching."

My great-great-grandfather William Corrie died in 1835, some 13 years after he had emigrated from Scotland to America. Over the decades the exact location of his grave was forgotten. His tombstone disappeared, and the little graveyard in which he was buried became overgrown with brambles.

As Dallas and I walked over that same ground, though, the witching wires gave no sign of pulling together. By the end of the day I realized that to find William, I would have to do more than tramp through a field that family lore had indicated was William's final resting place. If I wanted to find the William who had lived, I needed to go to Scotland, talk to the members of the Corrie family who were still in the ancestral homeland, visit the graves of those who were buried beneath it, and get to know about the people from William's past.

With no idea where the road would lead, I set out on what proved to be a fascinating, difficult, and ultimately rewarding adventure—my search for my long-lost relative William Corrie.

1. The Adventure Begins

The trail is the thing, not the end of the trail. Travel too fast and you miss all you are traveling for.

                                                    –Louis L'Amour

I n 1885 my grandfather, Thomas Newton Corrie, sat with his young family around the kitchen table in their small wood-frame house in eastern Illinois. My grandmother Nancy was moving back and forth from the cooking range to the table in a long calico dress. She had a faded blue apron tied around her waist, thickened by the bearing of five children. Her dark brown hair, streaked with gray, was pulled into a bun at the back of her head. In her work-worn hands she held a wooden spoon with which she stirred nourishing stew that bubbled in the cast-iron kettle on the stove. She ladled the steaming mixture of vegetables and meat into bowls and carried them, one at a time, to her waiting family. Then, she brought over the coffee pot and refilled her husband's cup. Thomas brushed the bread crumbs off his beard, settled his broad shoulders and muscular arms back in his chair, took a sip of coffee and smiled at his children quietly eating their stew, hoping their father would tell them a story.

"In southwest Scotland," Thomas began, "a beautiful rolling countryside borders Brighouse Bay. Up a gentle hill and facing the bay is a large manor house known as South Park. From its front steps you can look down to the bay which flows into the Irish Sea and then to the Atlantic Ocean. This house and the land around it came into the Corrie family in the 1700s. From it your great-grandfather William left Scotland to come to America with ten of his eleven children. One was an eight-year-old boy named Thomas. Eventually, Thomas became my father, your grandfather."

One of the children sitting at the kitchen table listening intently with a glass of fresh milk and thick slices of homemade bread before him was my father, Carl. He grew and matured in time and had a family of his own and passed these stories on to me and to Ruth, my older sister.

Thomas Newton Corrie and Nancy (Edmondson) Corrie's family—circa 1890. Clockwise from the left: Grace, Edgar, Roy, Ezra, Carl (Evelyn's father), mother Nancy, youngest son Frank, and father Thomas Newton Corrie.

I remember my father telling us, "William came to America in 1822, three years after his brother John found his way to Illinois. Six years later a third brother, Robert, came as well.

"William and his brothers were different than most immigrants. Their well-to-do brother Adam purchased 10,000 acres of land in Edwards County, Illinois, in 1817 and encouraged members of his family to go to America to settle on the land he had obtained. Adam gave John, William, and Robert money for preparations and to make the difficult journey across the ocean, hoping that each would better his station in life."

My father continued, "When William's son James was grown and married, a neighbor was jealous of his wife and family. She was so disagreeable many thought her to be a witch. Except for James and his son Henry, all of James's family died unexpectedly and the neighbor lady was accused of having poisoned them in a fit of jealous rage." Suddenly I wanted to know more. Witch or no witch, I wanted to know what tragedy actually befell James's family. Was this true or simply a story told to children?

Dad planted another thought in my mind. "Corrie family historians say our line goes back to Robert the Bruce. But then, most every true Scotsman and woman wishes that they were related to the great Scottish hero, too."

These and other declarations raised more questions. Why had William, my great-great-grandfather, left Scotland to come to the edge of the American wilderness? Had he read one of the many books popular at the time telling of the wondrous freedom and vast, bountiful land to be found there? Were times hard with low prices? Had he struggled to make a living for his large family? I wondered, too, did he have any notion of the hardship the long sea voyage would entail and the difficulties the family would experience on the overland trip to Pittsburgh and then floating down the Ohio River? What made them undertake this arduous journey when William was 57 and his wife Margaret 49, old for this period in the history of the world when such longevity was unusual? I had always imagined immigrants and homesteaders were young.

I had more questions than answers, but I intended to solve as many as I could.

Nancy Corrie's Stew

Nancy used the meat her family raised and vegetables from their garden to make tasty stews like this one.

2 pounds beef stew meat,
cubed
Water
1 teaspoon salt
1/3 cup rice

2 cups chopped onion
3 cups tomatoes
1 cup chopped celery
1 cup diced carrots
1 cup diced potatoes

Brown meat in a little shortening. Cover with water. Add salt, rice, and onions. Put on a lid and simmer 1 hour or until meat is tender. Skim any fat from top. Add vegetables to the broth and simmer for another 20 minutes, or until tender.

Genealogy Tip 1: Getting Started

Many authorities suggest starting a genealogical search with yourself, for you know most about your own background. However, I urge you to contact every living relative you can discover as soon as possible, especially the oldest members of your family, and ask for their input. The elderly are treasure troves of information and they may, like my father, leave our sides before we have learned all we wish from them. When I first began my research, I wrote letters to the oldest surviving Corries and encouraged them to answer soon and in as much detail as possible. I asked them to tell me what they knew of all the members of our scattered family.

I sent letters to the other relatives whose addresses I had, hoping to reach as many as possible before they, too, became simply names and numbers in my genealogy book. I discovered that some were living and some long gone. Those I wrote to knew of others, so my list of helpful relatives grew.

I visited those nearby, taking along my camera and my tape recorder. (Digital and video cameras are wonderful helps in doing interviews.) I always let them know I was coming, told them what I was looking for, and made an appointment to visit.

I soon discovered many delightful relatives I didn't know I had. The names, dates and stories they shared became the magic carpet necessary for my exciting journey.

2. Bits and Pieces

Patience, persistence, perseverance—the three p's of genealogy.
—*Iowa Genealogy Newsletter*

Fortunately for me, my father placed the bits and pieces of information he collected about my ancestors in his office file cabinet for safe keeping. Most of what he learned had come from the stories his father had told him and, later, from his mother Nancy and a cousin, Wallace Beals.

My most vivid memory of my grandmother Nancy is of an aging woman sitting in a wooden rocking chair. Her once tall, sturdy figure had become thin, shrunken, and frail. Her hands were blue-veined and gnarled with arthritis. She had her gray hair parted in the middle and pulled back into a bun at the back of her head in the simple style she had favored all her adult life. Although her eyes were bright blue as always, their blank appearance made her face look sad.

I was told that Nancy had lost her sight sometime in the 1920s due to a torn retina or glaucoma at a time when little could be done medically to correct those problems. As Grandma lived out the last twenty years of her life with her daughter Grace in the small adobe house in southeastern Colorado, I wonder what scenes she may have had in her mind behind those sightless eyes. Did she envision that small farm in Illinois which she and her family had left by covered wagon in 1886? Did she picture the place near Lewis, Kansas, where the family spent the following winter crowded in a dugout that, after they built their house, became the place where Nancy raised her chickens?

Nancy and her husband Thomas Newton Corrie erected a fine two-story frame home with a half-porch in the front where they could sit to rest in the evenings. Soon they had one more son to complete the family of five boys and one girl. I hope Nancy carried happy pictures in her mind of those days with her children learning and growing and helping on that busy ranch. What scenes could she still see of the time in 1903 when she and Thomas followed their daughter Grace into Colorado to homestead their last farm next to the one Grace had begun to "prove up?" No doubt Nancy remembered experiences she had that were similar to many pioneer families of that day who kept thinking they might improve their lot and have a more productive life if they just moved on west to better land.

Grace Corrie Doner's adobe house on the plains of southeastern Colorado, the final home of Evelyn's grandmother Nancy Corrie.

During my early visits to the adobe home in eastern Colorado where Grandma lived out the last years of her life, I very much enjoyed the time I spent with her granddaughter Olivia. The only daughter of my Aunt Grace, Olivia was my favorite cousin. Eleven months younger than I, we were our grandparents' youngest grandchildren, and we considered that a privilege. Olivia was a beautiful girl. Her sweet face, gentle manner, and soft rich voice contrasted with my more tomboyish, awkward actions and far less melodious speech, but we enjoyed one another's company and, despite the differences, were good friends.

Evelyn Corrie Birkby and her cousin, Olivia Doner, in 1930 on the step of Grace Doner's home near Walsh, Colorado. It is here that Nancy Corrie, Grace's mother, lived her final years.

I do not remember either Olivia or me getting any hugs from our grandmother or invitations to sit on her lap. Was her generation not as outwardly loving as those who came later, or was it just Nancy's way? She did welcome Olivia and me to come sit at her feet and I especially liked to hear her reminisce about "the olden days."

My father, however, proved to be the main recipient of information from my grandmother's store of memories. Dad was wise enough to write down everything his mother told him and filed the pieces of paper when he returned home. Later, when I held those notes in my hand, I was grateful for Dad's interest, for those scraps encouraged me to continue in my own search for family.

Nancy Corrie with her three minister sons: Roy, Carl (Evelyn's father) and Ezra. Circa 1930. By now Nancy was blind.

In addition to my grandmother's and cousin Olivia's materials, a large number of the papers in Dad's files came from information he received from a cousin, Wallace Beals. A genealogist who was deeply interested in the American branch of the Corrie family, Wallace had discovered my father on his family tree and wrote to Dad to start a rich friendship that became a great source of family records my father had not had before.

The summer of 1929, our family drove to central Illinois to visit my mother's kin. On the way back to our home in Iowa, we detoured to Rushville, Illinois, to meet Wallace Beals for the first time. He welcomed us warmly and then he said, "We need to go visit the Scripps sisters, Henrietta and Eliza. They are Corrie descendants just as we are and they want to meet you."

These maiden ladies lived together in a two-story white frame house set back from the road by a fine green lawn. They greeted us at their front door wearing modest, long, dark dresses, their hair pulled back into similar neat buns in the style of many women of their generation. The two were delighted to find new relatives to welcome into the family. They made pots of tea, brought out a tray of baked sweets, and put up with my childish enthusiasm as I roamed around their house poking my ten-year-old nose into every corner I could find.

Theirs was a fascinating house, with enough nooks and crannies to satisfy my childish curiosity. The rooms were large and the ceilings high. In the dining room was a wooden table with a surface so polished I could see my face in it. A sweet aroma drew me toward the kitchen where a work table covered with a red and white checkered table cloth held a platter of sugar cookies. I knew better than to take any without permission, but soon Henrietta came in to replenish the tray from the living room and smiled as she said, "Help yourself. I baked them just for you cousins. I made plenty, so eat all you want." She immediately became my favorite relative.

The room I enjoyed the most during our stay with the Scripps sisters was a turret where I spent much of that long afternoon imagining a prince and a princess inhabiting its circular space. What I didn't realize at the time was that this room's primary treasures were the sisters' records of the Corrie family.

My most vivid memory of that visit was the grandfather clock in the front hallway. It had a huge face dominated by a large sun that rose and set as the movement of the pendulum sent the minutes through the days and nights. Whenever I thought of that clock in later years, it seemed to be urging me to hurry with my research.

While I was exploring, Wallace, Eliza, Henrietta, and my father were sharing their genealogy resources. Wallace also told my father of the Corrie burials in the Terregles Cemetery not far from the town of Dumfries, Scotland. On a map Wallace pointed out the location of the Corrie lands near Kirkcudbright that included South Park. Dad made notes and took all the new information home where he added it to his Corrie file. From then on, Wallace sent my father more information whenever he found it.

As I grew older, each time I held Dad's file filled with the bits and pieces he had discovered of his family's history, I felt as if my ancestor William was beckoning to me. "Get to know me better. Learn about my roots—and yours—and put the pieces of the family puzzle together that have been fragmented for so long."

I realized that I needed to go to Scotland myself to see the land and learn firsthand all I could about my forebears.

By the time our three sons were grown I felt I could start saving for such a journey. I invited my husband and sons to go along, but they had their own education and careers to follow. Finally, with Dad's notes in my suitcase, I went looking for William alone.

Scripps Sisters' Sugar Cookies

Sharing sugar cookies is an excellent way to cement friendships. The Scripps Sisters shared their recipe, as well.

2 1/4 cups flour
1/4 teaspoon baking powder
1/4 teaspoon salt
1 cup butter

1/2 cup powdered sugar
2 Tablespoons milk
2 teaspoons vanilla flavoring

Combine dry ingredients. Set aside. Cream together the butter and powdered sugar; blend in milk and flavoring. Gradually add flour to mixture and mix well. Form into a ball, wrap in plastic wrap, and chill at least 30 minutes. Roll out portion of dough on a lightly floured board to 1/4 inch thick. Cut with a cookie cutter into the desired shapes. Repeat. Bake on an ungreased cookie sheet at 350 degrees for 8 to 10 minutes or until lightly brown around the edges. Cool.

Genealogy Tip 2: Keeping Track

When you begin copying down what you have learned, get family record sheets that you can carry with you to mark dates and names and information. It is wise to always carry a notebook in which you can write comments, locations, stories, and anything else that seems relevant to your search. When you return home you can type this information into whatever computerized family record program you are using.

Many genealogy programs are available and you need to find the one that works best for you. If some family members have already done research, you may want to use the same computer program they have so you will be consistent in numbering and terminology; sharing will be easier. Cyndi's List <*www.cyndislist.com*>, for example, has many resources and family record sheets available on the internet. Some can be printed off of web sites, or you can order materials from genealogical centers such as Everton Publishing Company in Logan, Utah.

Mark all information as to where you found it and with the name and address of the person who sent it to you, along with the date you received it. Store everything carefully in files so it won't get lost or cluttered. A file box for each line of the family is good if you don't own a regular file cabinet.

As I checked over the bits and pieces my father had filed from his experiences I was always pleased to find that he had dated them and marked where they originated and who had given him the information. Wallace Beals did the same. Every letter he received was carefully marked as to who the person was. He also made carbon copies (this was before the day of computers) of the letters he wrote back. Bits and pieces of the family story were in materials Wallace handed on to his grandson, Richard Corrie Beals, who in turn eventually loaned them all to me.

We who delve into genealogy can sometimes hit a dead end, and then the frustration begins. I started a folder for Corries unconnected to our family line and kept those notes, hoping someday to find a clue that would help make a connection.

Researching a family history is like going on a journey. It is a matter of taking one simple step after another, sometimes down an unknown path, to see where the road goes.

3. First Trip to Scotland

He who returns from a journey is not the same person as he who left.
—*Anonymous*

When I set off alone for Scotland at the age of 65, I carried a sturdy purse holding my passport, travelers' checks, a Britrail Pass and a charge card. I had packed several outfits into my small suitcase—two pairs of slacks (one red, one maroon), a black skirt suitable for formal affairs, three blouses and a sweater that could be mixed and matched with the other garments, plus the black travel outfit I wore as I boarded the plane in the States. I added a pair of warm pajamas, a lightweight nightgown, and three pairs each of undergarments. Who knew what weather I would experience? In a smaller bag I packed my makeup and some first aid items—a few Band-Aids and moleskin in case of blisters, medicine for an upset stomach, tablets in case I caught a cold, and a tube of antibiotic salve if I ran into anything like thorns or a cat that scratched or bit. I hoped the easy-to-pull wheeled trolley that carried my two bags and their contents would make me self-sufficient in my travels.

I took with me all the information Cousin Olivia had given me about her visit to the Dumfries area, the Terregles Cemetery, and the estate where South Park is located. She had given me names and addresses and maps and helped increase my sense of closeness with the people from my family's past. In addition, Cousin Wallace Beals had shared what he knew and letters from some Scottish locals. Now I had a place and an address and a need to go to the place where my ancestor William's story began.

Since I was traveling alone, I stopped in London for a few days to visit a friend of my son Bob and to get oriented to the unfamiliar signs, the interesting English accents, the narrow cobblestone streets, and the traffic coming at me from the wrong side of the road. Then at Euston Station I boarded the train bound for Dumfries, my first stop in Scotland.

The train was fast, clean, and on time. I liked it. Each pair of seats faced each other and were equipped with a good-size table in-between. A "stewardess" came by frequently, pushing a cart down the aisle between the seats, offering coffee and tea and snacks. A well-appointed dining car provided me with a delicious egg omelet and fresh hot coffee for an early lunch.

The sun was shining as we zipped through the English countryside. A canal with work and pleasure boats shared our landscape for a time. We flew past small villages with glimpses of neat, orderly rows of stone houses topped with chimney pots. Colorful flowers grew in the tiny yards.

By the time we reached the Lake District, a lovely young woman with bright, inquisitive eyes and a warm, friendly smile had taken the seat across the table from me. She introduced herself as Karen and explained, "I'm going to Dumfries to visit my aunt Margaret Brown. She and her husband Tom and two children live south of Dumfries in Kirkpatrick Durham."

When she heard my reason for traveling and that Dumfries was my destination, she said, "I'm certain Aunt Margaret will be happy to help you find a bed-and-breakfast for tonight." We watched out our shared window as the scenery grew increasingly rugged, sparsely populated and moor-like, with a quality both haunting and lonely. Suddenly, long lines of stone fences appeared. "When you see stone fences and flocks of black-faced sheep, you'll know you're in Scotland."

"Banners should be flying, bands should be playing, bells should be ringing!" I exclaimed. "I'm here!" Karen and I laughed together, savoring my joy. After years of hoping and months of planning, I felt I was finally getting close to William and the land and people who were an important part of his past.

The train stopped at Dumfries station right on time. "There she is!" Karen exclaimed as she waved to the person I knew was one of her favorite relatives. "Over here Aunt Margaret! I have someone I want you to meet."

The two hugged and shared greetings, and then I found myself in a warm embrace as well. Aunt Margaret was slight of build with dark brown hair and a kind, cheerful face. When Karen told her my story, Margaret smiled. "I can help you find a bed-and-breakfast, but why don't you come home with me and spend the night with my husband Tom and our family? Karen will be there too." Before I could say a word, she loaded my bags in her car, motioned for Karen to sit in the back, and ushered me into the front seat right beside her.

Margaret drove south toward Castle Douglas, a town I knew was on the way to my destination—Kirkcudbright—then up a winding narrow road to the quaint village of Kirkpatrick Durham. We stopped in front of a white house tucked between other white houses. The name Norwood painted over the door indicated to me permanence and a long existence. By the time we were out of the car, Margaret's son Andrew and daughter Susy were greeting us along with their short-haired brown and white terrier, Brownie.

Norwood, the house in the center of the photo, is Margaret and Tom Brown's home in Kirkpatrick Durham, were Evelyn spent her first night in Scotland. The Brown's niece, Karen is standing in the doorway

Margaret guided me into her well-kept living room and gestured for me to sit in a comfortable overstuffed chair near the fireplace. She disappeared into the kitchen and soon brought back a pot of hot tea, freshly-made cookies, and a square of fruit cake. As I began drinking the warm brew and nibbling on the tasty sweets, Margaret lit a peat fire in the hearth. Soon its glow made the chill wind and overcast skies seem distant. She poured herself a cup of tea and we sat visiting like old friends.

As she refilled my teacup she said, "I felt you should be in at least one ordinary home during your visit." I assured her that she had given me a treasure.

Before long, Margaret's husband Tom came home from work. If he was surprised at seeing a stranger in the house, he didn't show it. He smiled as he greeted me. Perhaps he was used to Margaret bringing home wandering strays from far away places.

Tom had a sturdy, muscular frame and a ruddy complexion that suggested years of working outdoors. As Margaret put together our evening meal he explained to me that he was a peat cutter and seller. The sign in his front window said "Galloway Peat for Good Heat."

"Business is good. People in this part of Scotland need fuel to ward off the cold winds that blow in from the sea." Just then, Margaret called us into the dining room. On the table was the main dish of cooked rice and kidney beans, something I had never eaten before but would learn to enjoy during my journey. Considering the fact that Margaret had not expected extra company, the meal was most generous and inviting.

Tom and Margaret Brown, who hosted Evelyn on her first trip to Scotland.

After we ate, we returned to the living room for another short visit where we found the fire had faded into glowing coals. Tom left the room for a minute and returned with a tiny glass. "Scots make the best whiskey in the world," he said. "I brought you a wee dram. This is my favorite from the Isle of Islay. Shall I cut it with a little water?"

"No, I'll try it the way you have it," I said courageously.

I took a tiny sip of what was a very strong, sturdy, "wee dram." As I wiped tears from my eyes and gulped to clear my burning throat, Tom and Margaret smiled encouragingly and I finally was able to croak, "Thank you. I should have accepted your offer to thin that drink with some water!"

It was after eleven o'clock when I finished telling them about my search for William and his family. I snuggled down into a comfortable bed, warmed underneath with an electric blanket and on top with a down comforter. I could not believe such a marvelous welcome was really happening. Why on earth had William ever left?

After a breakfast of what Margaret called "baps"—large, round buns as light as angel food cake inside and served with orange marmalade— we saw the two Brown children off to school. Margaret and Karen drove me to nearby Castle Douglas so that I could see about catching a bus to Kirkcudbright, but Margaret's friendly machinations were not yet complete. She drove past the last house in Kirkpatrick Durham, through Castle Douglas, and on down the road, taking me all the way to my destination.

As I enjoyed the hilly countryside I said to her, "We are near where a relative, John Corrie, lives. It is called Park of Tongland and I understand it is on the way to Kirkcudbright. I wrote to John telling him I would be in the area and would like to meet him."

Margaret smiled, "We are close to the Park of Tongland now." She pulled off the main road and with my assistance found John and Sandra Corrie's fine manor house at the end of a lane. Sadly, neither Corrie was at home that day so I did not get to see them, but their maid handed me a small piece of paper containing the name and address of the premiere British Corrie family historian, James Corrie, who lived in Burgess Hills, Sussex, England. I tucked that scrap of paper into my billfold, knowing I would carry it all the way back across the ocean to put into the file of information that had been started by my father.

Kirkcudbright (pronounced a soft purring "Ka-COOO-bree") is a quiet, picturesque fishing village located at the mouth of the River Dee which flows into Kirkcudbright Bay. Rows of whitewashed cottages nestle low as if they expect at any moment a howling north wind will sweep down upon them—something which may, indeed, happen during the winter months in this seaside town.

John Corrie of Park of Tongland, and two of his Belted Galloway cattle. Photo from Kent Tool.

Karen, Margaret, and I stopped at the Tourist Information Centre where an attendant located a room for me in a former bank building, now called The Bank Bed-and-Breakfast. After we drove there and carried my luggage upstairs into my room, Margaret and I, regretfully, said good-bye.

I unpacked my bags and told myself that if the Browns were an example of the Scottish people, I would soon love this country. The next day I wrote Margaret a note thanking her for her kindness and told her how delighted I was that she had helped me find James Corrie's address.

Then it was time for me to find South Park, the country manor home from which my great-great-grandfather and his family had emigrated four generations before.

Margaret Brown's Scottish Baps

The traditional breakfast bread Margaret Brown served me for my first breakfast in Scotland was so light and airy that it seemed as though it could float away.

(Light Rolls)
1/2 cup milk
2 teaspoons sugar
1 teaspoon salt

1/4 cup butter or lard
1 envelope yeast
1/2 cup lukewarm water
3 1/2 cups flour

Scald milk.(Heat until bubbles form around the edge.) Remove from fire. Add sugar, salt and butter or lard. Stir to dissolve and set aside to cool to lukewarm. Dissolve yeast in lukewarm water in a large, warmed bowl (rinse bowl with hot water to warm). Add lukewarm milk mixture. Beat in half the flour. When very smooth, stir in remaining flour—just enough to make a soft dough. Knead lightly a minute or two. Put in greased bowl, grease top of dough, cover and set in a warm place to rise until double in bulk—about 1 hour.

Turn dough onto floured board and knead lightly for 2 minutes. Cut into 12 portions. Shape each portion into an oval about 3 inches long and 2 inches wide. Put on greased baking sheet so the ovals do not touch. Brush tops with milk. Cover with a tea towel and let rise until double in bulk. Do not hurry this rising. Bake at 400 degrees for 15 to 20 minutes. Perfect when eaten with butter and orange marmalade.

Genealogy Tip 3: Helpful Attitudes

As I traveled alone in Britain at age 65, I learned to be flexible, to expect the unexpected, and to always carry food!

FLEXIBILITY is the key to enjoying everything that happens. Even when I had no idea how I was going to get from one place to another, I found someone who was glad to help me. In Britain every town of any size has an information-tourist centre where helpful people have lists of bed-and-breakfast lodgings, and information about historical places.

EXPECT THE UNEXPECTED is a good motto for whatever search you are undertaking. This way you will never be caught off guard if some things don't go exactly as planned. I found that trains in Scotland may not run on certain days, but that gave me time to go to a village festival, or take a tour bus to a local place of interest, or roam in and out of back streets and alleyways to find interesting shops, ornate churches, and charming tea houses.

Be prepared for frustrations such as that I experienced when I did not find John and Sandra Corrie at home. The plus side, of course, was the information they left with their maid. A genealogist must have a positive attitude. Expect the successes to overshadow the disappointments, and most of all, have fun!

ALWAYS CARRY FOOD. My sons warn people that those who value their lives should never tamper with their mother's feeding schedule. And they are right! I need food to keep my energy level at its peak. When I get hungry I get grumpy. Thus, I learned early on to take a snack with me in case I found myself in a genealogy library, or in a back street, or on a bus where food was not available. That became my third "given" in my rules for successful travel. A candy bar, a little package of cheese crackers, a piece of fruit, anything that will carry you through until more substantial sustenance can be found, is essential to a great travel experience.

4. Finding South Park

All their stones and all their accomplishments sit atop the stones of their mothers and fathers, stone upon stone, beneath the waters of their lives.

—Mitch Albom, *The Five People You Meet in Heaven*

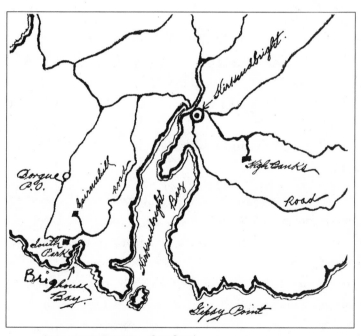

Area near Borgue, Scotland bordering on Brighouse Bay Includes South Park and Cairniehill

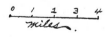

S oon after breakfast my first morning in Kirkcudbright, I looked for a way to travel the seven miles west to the Corrie estates. The community had no taxi. "But we have a post bus," my bed-and-breakfast host told me. "The mailman drives out every morning and takes paying passengers."

"It sounds like an interesting way to travel your countryside," I said, "but I imagine it is a roundabout way to go and I might find it hard to get back. Do you know of anyone who would drive me out? A retiree perhaps? My Cousin Olivia told me that was the way she had gone to South Park during her visit to Scotland."

"There's Mr. McMinn across the street. He's retired and often drives people places. He knows Douglas Gillespie, the owner of South Park, He'd probably enjoy visiting with him."

I knocked on Samuel McMinn's door and was greeted with a smile by a tall, slender, gray-haired gentleman. When I told him who I was he said, "I remember your cousin Olivia. Sure, I'd be glad to take you to South Park." Soon I was in Mr. McMinn's small car. Off we went up the hills and down the hills, around curves and corners, over bridges and footpaths, and under leafy arches that the trees formed over our heads.

Mr. McMinn's first stop was in the village of Borgue where he had also taken Olivia. We parked by a small square-towered Norman church standing guard over a cemetery. Some of the stones were tall, dark, ancient and moss-covered. Others were fresh and new. An iron railing sectioned off one large area which held a memorial over six-feet high upon which were painted the names of many of the Corries who had not come to America and were buried in their native soil. I took several photographs so later I could sort out all those names and dates. I wanted to know how each was related to my ancestor William, but Mr. McMinn had no idea.

We drove along the country roads to a rock-enclosed drive that led us to a Corrie farm known as Cairniehill. Near the top of a hill, surrounded by trees and several stone outbuildings, stood a house with walls of gray rock built generations ago and purchased in 1778 by an uncle of my ancestor, William. Now, 200 years later, Douglas Gillespie's hired dairy man lives in the old house and when he saw us, he came outside.

Cairniehill house.

"This is rich grassland for dairy cows," he explained to me. "Mr. Gillespie has many cows that I care for and milk. The new building hidden behind the old house is now the dairy barn."

We waved good-bye, and as we drove back down the Cairniehill lane, my sense of excitement increased. These were the same roads William had ridden on and walked as a boy in the late 1700s with his Father John, his mother Margaret, and his brothers and sister when they all lived at South Park.

Cairniehill house. Aerial view of Cairniehill with dairy barns in the rear. Photo from Gladys Corrie Illingworth.

We went up and down and around a few more miles of roads bordered with stone walls. Our route took us through Corrie land all the way, with uneven ridges beside the road indicating a rocky subsoil. We glimpsed Brighouse Bay with its deep blue waters reaching to the horizon. A hill across the bay held a house I later learned had once belonged to the Corries.

Mr. McMinn slowed the car near an old mill house. Nearby, at the top of a gentle rise, was the entrance of the three-story house known as South Park. Its walls were softened by graceful green ivy growing partway up the walls. The windows and doors were outlined in blue. The effect was dignified and elegant.

Before I left the States I had written to Douglas Gillespie, the current owner of the home and property, who had married Mary Isabella Corrie and thus had, upon her death, inherited these Corrie lands. He was expecting me and met us at the door. He was as fragile and genteel as the house in which he lived. "Come in," he said. "You are

South Park manor house near Borgue, Scotland. Original painting by Harlan Corrie.

most welcome. I understand you are trying to learn more about your ancestor William Corrie. Perhaps you can tell me about the people who went to America as well. By all means, come in."

We walked past antique furnishings and over the thick carpet, its colors muted by generations of feet, and stepped into the sitting room where Mr. McMinn, Mr. Gillespie, and I drew up comfortable chairs near the fireplace.

It was a joy to sit and absorb the beauty of the home, the warmth of the fire, and my host's friendliness. We talked of his wife, who died in 1972. "I've read some of her letters and know stories of others who have visited South Park from America," I told him.

"Yes, we've had many visitors here over the years and Isabella always enjoyed every one them. I wish you could have met her." I mentioned what I knew of the Corries who lived in this place and of those, including my ancestor William, who left. As we visited, Mr. McMinn told Douglas the current news of mutual friends in the village.

When it was time for tea, Douglas's housekeeper slipped into the room with a plate of dark-brown ginger-bread, golden almond cakes, and a pot of strong, hot tea. Mr. Gillespie removed the hand-beaded tea cozy from the pot. The teapot was decorated with flowers and birds with a thick outline of gold, as was the cup he handed to me.

Mr. McMinn (on the left) and Mr. Gillespie, pouring tea in the South Park parlor.

Mr. Gillespie made me think of many descriptions I'd read of proper

British gentlemen. He was short in stature with delicate features and an energy to his voice and movements that belied his stooped shoulders and graying hair. In my mind I framed the scene of him pouring the tea as if this were his favorite ritual. It was too special a moment to forget.

When it was time to leave, I stepped outside and looked across the wide, verdant green pastures reaching out to the water of Brighouse Bay. "I wish I knew how my William felt in 1822 as he left his father and mother knowing he would never return," I told Mr. Gillespie. "How strong he must have been to travel so far away to a land he had never seen. I think this place and its people were part of the reasons he was courageous enough to make the journey. Thank you for sharing your home and stories with me." I stepped off the well-worn stone step and waved one last time at Mr. Gillespie as he waved back from the door of South Park.

As we drove away, I wondered aloud where I should go next. Stopping in front of the Kirkcudbright bus station, Mr. McMinn asked, "Have you thought of going to the research library in Edinburgh?" Sure enough, early the next morning a bus was scheduled that could get me to Edinburgh and its genealogy center. Yes, I decided, that was where I was going next to learn more about William and his family.

South Park Gingerbread

Whenever I eat gingerbread, I remember the happy visit I made to South Park.

3 cups flour
2 teaspoons ground ginger
1 teaspoon soda
2/3 cup currents or raisins
2/3 cup blanched, chopped
    almonds

1/2 cup vegetable shortening
1/2 cup dark corn syrup
1/2 cup dark molasses
1/2 cup sugar
1/2 cup milk
1 large or 2 small eggs

Sift dry ingredients together into bowl; stir in currents or raisins and nuts. Heat together the shortening, syrup, molasses, and sugar until dissolved. Cool. Combine milk and lightly beaten egg, add to heated mixture alternately with flour mixture, stirring with a wooden spoon (batter will be thick.)

Grease a bread pan, cover the bottom of the pan with waxed paper, and grease the paper. Spread batter in pan and bake at 375 degrees for 35 minutes or until gingerbread tests done. Let cool in pan for 10 minutes, then turn out on rack. This may also be baked in an 8-inch square pan following same directions given. (All the gingerbread I ate on my journey had been baked in a standard bread pan.)

Genealogy Tip 4:
Importance and Care of Photographs

Photographs can be an important part of your research. Photos of people, places, cemetery stones, and special records can give you valuable material to be used in a variety of ways. They can prove you were in a certain place at a certain date. Tombstones can give you additional records of dates and names. Photos of family groups can identify who belongs in which family line.

When you take photographs, be sure to number the pictures and identify them in a notebook. Write down the place and names and anything pertinent so you will have a record. Use black ink in case you want to photocopy your information. On the back of pictures use a photo marking pen or a soft lead pencil.

Old photographs are of special value in learning about your relatives. With luck, someone will have already marked them with a date, place and name. If not, write on the back any information you may find that might help you later. If you aren't sure of your facts, you can add a note that your information is only a guess.

Photographs should always be kept in archival safe sleeves, albums, or scrapbooks. Many local office supply stores carry archival-safe supplies and can help you find what you need. Keep photographs out of the light as much as possible to prevent them from fading. Computer scanners are a good way to make duplicates to share with relatives and to protect the originals.

When I travel I always take a notebook that fits in my purse. I find it useful for writing down new information, names and addresses of people who helped me, and notes about pictures. I also use the notebook as a journal for writing about my experiences as they happen.

5. Off to Edinburgh

We live with a heritage from earlier generations and must seek to create positive legacies for those who follow us. When the old are not allowed to tell their story, the young grow up without history. If the young are not listened to, we have no future.

–Dr. Gunhild O. Hagostad

It was early morning and the air was crisp and cool as I pulled my wheeled luggage down the street from the bed-and-breakfast where I had just finished eating a traditional Scottish breakfast of thick bacon, eggs, tomatoes, and toast served in a cooling rack. (The British like their toast crisp and think that placing pieces together makes them soggy.) My plate also held a serving of blood pudding which I did not eat. Somehow, despite the fact that I had vowed to try anything a menu offered, that black congealed patty did not appeal to me that early in the morning.

I felt sad at leaving Kirkcudbright, where my ancestors had walked. I thought of William as I passed the ruins of the 16th century castle and the historic tollbooth building. He would have seen those buildings when he was on this street. At 7:15 a.m. in the late 20th century, the only sign of life I saw on the street was the local dairyman going about his appointed rounds. He paused long enough to leave a pint glass bottle filled with milk in front of the depot door.

The bus I planned to take from Kirkcudbright to Dumfries was scheduled to leave at 7:30 a.m. and make a connection there with a bus to Edinburgh after a 25-minute layover. No one was near the bus station as the time of departure grew close, and I became increasingly uneasy. Finally, I knocked on the depot door and a gentleman opened it. "Which is the bus to Dumfries?" I asked. He acted as if everything was on schedule as he pointed toward one of the buses. "That one," he told me and, seemingly unhappy to have been interrupted, shut the door before I could ask him where I should pay for my ticket.

As I stepped aboard the bus, several other passengers appeared. At exactly 7:30, the driver arrived, climbed into his seat, shut a low gate which separated him from the travelers, then proceeded to take our fares. Once this task was done, he closed the bus door and off we went.

The bus stopped along the road wherever people were waiting. The driver picked up farmers with tools, workmen with lunch pails, a woman with a white dog in her arms, ladies with shopping bags, and school children dressed in uniforms, the colors of their blazers identifying their schools. I was sure that before the day was over they would all catch the bus for the ride back to where they started.

The bus reached Dumfries, passed the statue of the poet Robert Burns, and coasted into a large parking lot with no station or waiting room. A small building nearby featured a sign that said *TOILET* and doors labeled *MEN* and *WOMEN*. Not *LAVATORY*, or *LOO* or *WATER CLOSET*. No *LADS* and *LASSIES*. Practical people these Scots, I thought to myself, where they call a toilet a toilet!

Back in the parking lot a gentleman wearing a small pin on his shirt identifying him as the bus dispatcher. "Can you direct me to the bus to Edinburgh?" I inquired.

"That one. Number 12," he said. Despite the fact that it said *Dum-fries* on the front, I loaded my luggage into Number 12, then popped across the street to get a cup of coffee to go.

By the time I returned, other travelers were getting on the bus, and as we drove away the sign on the front of the bus still said *Dumfries*. "I will not worry," I told myself. "I have faith in a man with 'Dispatcher' written on his chest."

The bus went through the Moorfoots, the Pentlands, and the Southern Uplands. Around every bend in the road was a surprise and joy: ruins of an ancient castle, a regal manor house flanked by forests, a village of tiny white stone cottages with smoke curling from their chimneys, flower beds in every wee front yard, and town squares holding small memorials from long ago. In some communities the long, gray lines of government-built low-rent housing looked cold and barren compared to the homey Scottish cottages.

The rolling hillsides were exceedingly green, nurturing many sleek black and white cows and long-wooled white sheep with black faces. The hills gradually became more mountainous and the trees more sparse. The highway was narrow and winding, the pace of the bus leisurely. It was a delightful way for me to absorb Scotland in minute detail. The sun shown, the sky was a deep blue, and I was content.

The bus driver did not call out the name of any of the villages where he stopped to allow passengers to alight or climb aboard. I got out my map, matched its symbols to the road signs we were passing, and was soon able to track our route toward Scotland's capitol city.

It was almost noon when we neared the city of Edinburgh. My excitement increased when I saw Edinburgh Castle on the rugged cliffs overlooking the city. It struck me as amazingly grim, a forbidding fortress centuries old and steeped in the history of the country.

The bus brought us into the central part of the city with its spires and squares, business houses and shops. It stopped near St. Andrew's Square and I emerged into the bustling heart of this gem of Scotland's cities. I had plenty of time to eat lunch, find a place to spend the night, then learn where the genealogy research library was located.

Pulling my luggage along behind me, I stepped into a hotel to inquire if they might have a room. "No," the kind lady at the desk told me. "Try next door."

"No," said the gentleman at the desk of the second hotel. He was busy and brusque but he did telephone another hotel on the street to discover that they did have an available room.

When I got to the Mount Royal Hotel and went up the elevator from the ground floor to the first floor (I was learning more about the vernacular of Scotland all the time) I found the desk clerk waiting for me. "We had a tour group cancel so we have a nice room with a window that looks out on the Firth of Forth. I can let you have it for the same price the tour people were going to pay."

The hotel was right on Princes Street, the main thoroughfare in the city of Edinburgh. A *firth*, I learned, is an estuary, and the one I could see from my window was part of the River Forth. I admired the expanse of deep blue water and the graceful Firth of Forth Bridge that carries traffic to and from the Highlands. Then I turned away from the view to explore the rest of my room.

Atop a small chest of drawers was an electric tea kettle. Beside it was a basket with sealed envelopes of tea bags and instant coffee along with sugars and creamers. Two tea cups stood beside the kettle ready for any pick-me-ups spots of brew I might desire.

In the adjoining bathroom, beside a tub that seemed as large as the cruise liner *Queen Mary*, was an upside-down U-shaped pipe through

Firth of Forth bridge, Edinburgh, Scotland. From Fremont County, Iowa, Historical Society collection.

which hot water flowed. Draped over the pipe was my bath towel, warm and cozy. I realized at once that this would be the perfect place to hang any clothing I laundered in the sink. The wet garments would dry rapidly in the warmth radiating from the pipe.

I didn't linger long in my room. I was hungry and about to discover pub lunches. British pubs are gathering places for far more than just those who wish to drink a pint or two of ale. People come to pubs to visit with neighbors and friends, to share news, and to eat simple, well-made meals.

As I walked around the corner from my hotel I saw a blackboard advertising the day's lunch at a nearby pub. The place looked friendly and inviting. I went down five steps below street level and entered a large room filled with tables that were all taken. A young woman eating alone motioned for me to join her. She had a warm smile and her fair skin, bright red hair, and dark blue eyes were similar to the features of many of the Scots I had seen on my journey.

"I want to know who you are and what you are doing here alone in the middle of Edinburgh," she said as I pulled up a chair.

"Hoping to get lunch," I answered. My new friend told me I needed to go up to the bar to put in my order. I did as she directed and chose an intriguing sounding dish—Colcannon. As I ate the delicious combination of fresh garden vegetables, I told my tablemate of my quest.

Her eyes sparkled with delight. "I'm so glad to know that you are roaming around by yourself," she remarked. "I thought when I reached 50 I'd be done with adventure and here you are, 65 years old, and traveling like a teenager. I still want to be experiencing new things when I am your age." When we were finished eating, I thanked her, she gave me a hug, wished me well, and sent me on my way.

Now well-fed and happy, I started out to explore the city. I spent three days in Edinburgh and, yes, within walking distance of my hotel, I found the famous Edinburgh Genealogical Research Centre.

Edinburgh has long been a place of excellence for Scottish historical and family research. It holds records which date back to the early 16th Century. For a time the country's politicians did not keep records but, thank goodness, the parish churches did, very carefully and sometimes secretly. The Old Parish Records (OPRs), which date from 1553 to 1854, contain information on births, baptisms, marriages, and deaths. Many are preserved on microfilm.

The Research Centre collections are stored in a weathered stone building at the east end of Princes Street across from the railroad hotel. Warm and friendly inside, the Research Centre held the records of the lives of many people. The morning of my first full day in the city I walked through the entrance doors, followed the signs and arrows to the information desk, and was directed to the area where the librarian got out a microfilm from the 1700s from Borgue Parish. I cheerfully paid the £5 rental fee.

The large reading room to which this helper directed me had an impressive dome over some 50 study spaces holding microfilm readers. I was surprised to see several pillows on top of the tables but I kept from suggesting that they might be in readiness for my weary head in case I nodded. When I asked the researcher at the room's information desk their purpose she told me, "Many of our old books are fragile, so we require patrons to lay them on the pillows we've provided." Her explanation made perfect sense.

My excitement mounted as I fed my film into the reader and I saw pictures of pages from the Borgue parish records. The neat script written by the priests and ministers looked ancient. I was grateful to the pastors who had made those artistic, graceful letters and numbers denoting births, baptisms, marriages and deaths. I discovered the delicately-worded terminology for babies. Those born to married couples were listed as "lawful children." Ones born out of wedlock were listed as "natural children."

I had trouble with some of the old script, but the longer I read it, the more I understood. I found familiar names, dates, and places, and I copied down the ones that were connected with my family. Suddenly leaping from the pages was my William. "Born the eldest child of John Corrie and his wife, Margaret Thomson, baptized 5 Apr 1766; married in Borgue 31 July 1794 to Margaret Gracey (or Gracie) who was born 1773 in Borgue."

I sat for a time absorbing the joy and wonder of finding my great-great-grandfather in these records and verifying his existence. Returning my attention to the film reader, I realized that the sunny room was warm and I was having trouble keeping the lower range of my bifocals aimed at the screen. My eyes became teary, making the words blur. I had a crick in my neck from the angle I had to hold my head to read. Then I remembered that I had not eaten for a long time and I was growing hungry. Hunger is never helpful when one is doing research.

It was at that moment I discovered that I was not particularly good at the deep inquiry of a true genealogist.

It takes a great deal of patience to dig into old dusty files, and record details of names and dates and places. It takes fortitude to spend long hours checking and rechecking data. It takes a willingness to accept disappointment when a lead turns into a dead end. And it takes planning around meal schedules so hunger does not interrupt research.

I gathered my papers and removed the microfilm from the reader, reluctant to return the historical record of William to its diligent owners. When I placed the film on the desk, I knew I needed to contact the relative who was my family's most serious researcher. What I had to do was to find James Corrie.

Colcannon

Cabbages are grown in Scotland, as well as turnips, potatoes, and carrots. The thrifty Scots put these vegetables together in this hearty dish.

1 small head cabbage   1 small turnip
2 carrots   2 Tablespoons butter
4 medium potatoes   Salt and pepper to taste

Shred cabbage and simmer with a little water until tender. Drain. In another pan, simmer remaining vegetables which have been peeled and cubed, using a minimum of water. Combine with cabbage and butter and season as desired. Drain and mash together for a surprising variation on mashed potatoes.

Genealogy Tip 5: Research Helps

When you head for a research center you need to take with you your record sheets, black ink pens, and a notebook. Parish records, census lists, family history centers such as those staffed by the Latter Day Saints, county historical societies, county court houses, and libraries are good places for research.

Church records contain evidence of baptisms, deaths and marriages. If you know the name and location of a parish where your ancestors lived you can write to the church and ask for information about specific people.

Census records come in a variety of forms. Some are on microfilm in libraries, others are on the internet. Both of these are important primary sources. Examine spellings carefully. Census takers often wrote down what they thought they heard, so sometimes the spelling is phonetic.

Local historians, library assistants, and professional genealogists may be available to help with your research. Be prepared to pay for their services, as their work is time-consuming and the material they find is often priceless. If you don't know where to find someone to help you, ask your state historical society for a reference.

When doing research, take along the name (or names) of those you want to research, their maiden names, surnames, any dates you have for those people, where they lived, their parents' names, dates of births or baptisms, dates and places of deaths. Writing down what you already know about a person will save you time when you get to a research center. Plan ahead and let the local historians know you are coming. This will give them time to check their records for information before you arrive.

Study the way your family name has been spelled through the generations. My father always said if the name was spelled Corrie, that person was related to us, but I have found Curries, Corys, Cories, and Korys who claimed kinship as well.

6. A London Meeting

. . . what the next generation will value most is not what we owned, but the evidence of who we were and the tales of how we loved. In the end, it's the family stories that are worth the storage.

—Ellen Goodman

It was several years before I was able to return to Britain and meet James Corrie, the goldmine of my family's history. I had kept his address in my files since the day Margaret Brown drove me to the home of Sandra and John Corrie at Park of Tongland. I had corresponded with James and now, along with my son Craig and his wife Sharon, we headed for London and the Park Lane Hotel where James suggested a day when he could come from his home in Sussex to visit.

James Corrie arrived on a bright sunny morning as Craig and Sharon went off to explore Westminster Abbey. When he walked through the door I immediately knew who he was. Tall, lean, and rugged in appearance with blue eyes, a broad smile, and a fringe of white hair around the back of his head, he looked as familiar to me as many of the men with whom I had grown up. He was definitely a Corrie.

We sat on a comfortable sofa in the lobby. A hotel waiter brought us salmon and cucumber sandwiches and, at James' request, gunpowder tea. "That's my favorite kind," he told me. "Workers roll the leaves into tiny balls that look like pellets of gunpowder." I took my first sip of the dark green liquid expecting it to go off like a sky rocket in my mouth,

James Corrie with Evelyn in the lobby of the Park Lane Hotel, London.

only to find it more like a delicate sparkler. From that day on I have searched out gunpowder tea at every opportunity and think of my visit with James as I drink it.

Over lunch James looked at me with the expression of someone who has much to share and is delighted to find someone who will listen. The crinkles around the edges of his eyes added emphasis to his excited smile as he began to tell me about himself. "I was born in Ilford, Essex, England. When I grew up I became a newspaper circulation manager and moved to Burgess Hill, West Sussex. I was married in 1941 and have three sons." His eyes brightened and his smile broadened as he turned the conversation to Jessie Corrie, the woman who inspired him to become a family historian.

"In the late 1800s Jessie gathered together what she could find on the Corries and in 1898 published her findings in a large book she called *Records of The Corrie Family.* In it she included stories as far back to Robert the Bruce in her effort to tie our family into his. She also included her own childhood stories and as much as she knew about the three brothers who emigrated to America.

"A valuable part of her book, " James continued, "is a drawing of the cemetery in Terregles near Dumfries. She included a map of the graves of the earliest Corrie ancestors." James continued to talk about his contacts with Jessie, while I scribbled as fast as I could in my notebook, trying to get down every word.

"I started corresponding with Jessie in 1938 regarding the Terregles families. She examined my records but was unable to find anything not already in her book."

"Did you get to know her personally?"

"Oh yes, I was so interested in her research that I decided I needed to go meet her, but first, unfortunately, I had to go to war.

"Jessie was clairvoyant. During the First World War her home, the Elms, a small mansion near Winchester, was used as a hospital for wounded soldiers and Jessie served as a nurse. She was a talented artist and drew a battle scene from her imagination. One of her soldier patients asked how she could have drawn so correctly many of the details.

JESSIE E. CORRIE. (1897.)

Jessie E. Corrie picture from the front of her Corrie History book. Contributed by James Corrie.

"In the summer of 1941, I was stationed for several months at Alresford, six miles from Itchen-Abbas, Hampshire, where Jessie lived. I was a private in the London Scottish Regiment. I had one day off each week, and alternate weeks I went home to Ilford in Essex and the other weeks I worked as casual laborer on a local farm to earn the money for the fare home.

"One morning, while dressing in my farm clothes, I thought 'I ought to visit Jessie!' So I put on my kilt and polished boots and tramped to Itchen-Abbas. Her maid, Theodora, answered the door and strangely, she seemed to be expecting me. She explained that Jessie spent most of her days in bed and was asleep but was hoping to see me when she awoke in the afternoon. Now I began to believe in her clairvoyance.

"Lunch was ready and waiting, so I ate. When I was done, Theodora asked if I would like to have a look around. The house was full of treasures; oil paintings, drawings and photographs, most all Jessie's work, wood and ivory furnishings and textiles made by various members of the family, all of superb craftsmanship.

"When I saw Jessie at about 3 p.m. she said she was glad I had been able to come and would I please believe she could see things others could not. She urged me to beware of being under a tree. What sort of tree she did not say, but reiterated her warning, struggling to raise her head from the pillow. She was then about 86 years old, and indeed looked older. I was 27.

"As a soldier I spent a lot my time under trees, as they were a protection from aircraft. It was wartime and a soldier's life was a busy one. I soon forgot about Jessie's warning."

"Did her caution ever come true?" I asked, feeling goose bumps rise over my skin.

"About three and a half years later," he said, "while searching in the gloom of a dense Burmese forest, I saw in a large clearing a heap of debris left by the retreating Japanese, including a dozen fencing masks. Hoping to find a souvenir sword, I strode purposefully forward. Suddenly, in mid-step, for no reason, I became alarmed. I crouched down and looked around. I was alone and could not explain a sudden feeling of being watched.

"I noticed the clearing in the undergrowth was caused by an enormous tree which created a canopy, then I remembered Jessie's warning. I quickly turned around and left. I cannot say whether danger lurked there, but I didn't think it my duty to find out."

James sipped his tea and said, "This happened in January, 1945. Jessie died in early March."

James told me how Adam, one my ancestor William's brothers, earned a fortune that eventually made it possible for three of his brothers to come to America. "In the late 1700s, Brother Adam and his Uncle William had mule trains that carried lace goods into Scotland from north of London, then returned to England laden with Scottish goods. This is the source of the money that Adam used to buy land in Illinois."

After we finished the last of our sweets, James laid a copy of his research on the family in my lap. It contained all James had discovered about the family, including a listing of the British members and those who had left for New Zealand, South Africa, and Australia.

"Is my William in your book?" I asked James.

James Corrie in the lobby of the Park Lane hotel getting acquainted with his American relatives, left to right: Sharon Birkby, Evelyn, James Corrie and Craig Birkby.

"Yes, everything I have learned about the three brothers who went to America is there," he answered. "But you need to add stories about what happened after they arrived." James gave me a delightful Corrie smile. "Stay in touch. I will help you in any way I can."

I gave James a loving hug and, with one last thank you, watched as he went out the door of the Park Lane Hotel. I was sad to think I might never see him again, but delighted with his gift of family. I clutched his blue bound book containing Jessie's map of Terregles and its graveyard, and I started to plan my next visit to Scotland.

Cucumber Sandwiches

Everywhere I went in the British Isles I found cucumber sandwiches. Some were simply sliced cucumbers layered on paper-thin slices of buttered bread. For a gourmet delight, cucumbers were sometimes sliced and combined with other vegetables, mayonnaise, and cream cheese and served on homemade bread.

1 small onion, grated
2 stalks celery, finely diced
1 8-ounce package cream cheese
  (room temperature)

1 medium cucumber, peeled and
  sliced thin
Mayonnaise and butter

Combine all ingredients except for cucumbers, mayonnaise and butter. Spread bread with butter and mayonnaise. Spread filling mixture over bread and make a layer of cucumber slices on top. Salt if desired. These can be made into open-faced sandwiches or you can spread butter and mayonnaise on another slice of bread and place on top for a full presentation.

Genealogy Tip 6: Sharing Information

It is a great help if your family has a careful researcher. If yours does not have one, perhaps you can fill that role. It is also possible to find people who, for a fee, will do research for you. That is particularly helpful in far off places where it may be difficult to travel.

James, our British family historian had not only shared his material with me, he also introduced me to Jessie Corrie, an even earlier researcher and writer. Her book, published in 1899, speculated that our family line extended back to Robert the Bruce, and provided a picture and story of the Corrie coat of arms.

James imbued me with his enthusiasm for the project. He made me want to hop on the next plane home to find out all I could about the people who came to America from the old country, and add their stories to Jessie and James' research. I clutched his blue notebook to my chest and felt as if he had just given me the honor of being one in a line of important family historians.

Keeping up one's enthusiasm is important. Research can take a long time and be tedious. At times it seems as if it can go on forever. Try not to be discouraged if people you think should help tell you they are too busy. Perhaps they will later find the time to get back to you, especially if you stay in touch with them.

Even though young people may not be initially interested in genealogy, many families find that when their children grow up and have children of their own, they want to know about their ancestors. Keep them informed about what you are doing; tell them interesting narratives about their kin and hope that the stories will stay in their minds and eventually be passed along to future generations.

I told James of my concern about making errors. "I worry about having my book in print and then finding something wrong, dates, or spelling, or names and places."

"Don't worry about it," he reassured me. "Once you have your material in print where others have a chance to look at it carefully from their knowledge, if they find errors they'll tell you. If you never printed the material, whatever mistakes you might make would never be corrected."

7. Terregles

I spent more time in cemeteries with my mother in Scotland than I will spend in one after I am dead.

—*Bob Birkby*

When my son Bob asked me what I wanted for my 75th birthday he thought I would say a waffle iron or a new toaster. But I didn't. I told him, "What I want more than anything, is for you and your brothers to go with me to Scotland. I want to take you where I found some of our heritage, and see if we can find more of the missing pieces of our family history I have been putting together to learn more about William."

Two sons, Bob and Jeff, accepted my offer. Son Craig, busy with his medical practice and his family, could not spare the time for travel, and my husband Robert opted to stay home as well.

This trip took a different turn than the one I had made earlier by train and bus. The three of us flew into Glasgow and rented a car. Bob drove on what felt like the wrong side of the road. Jeff navigated, and I sat in the back seat with the Corrie genealogy book on my lap reading aloud anything that related to the land through which we were traveling.

As we rode south of Glasgow, the flat countryside gradually dissolved into rolling hills covered with lush, emerald-green grass.

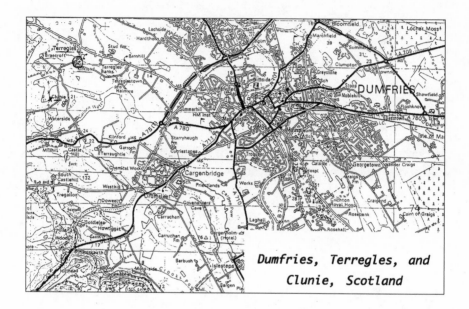

Dumfries, Terregles, and Clunie, Scotland

Black-faced sheep, fat with fine fodder and covered with thick white wool, dotted the landscape. The ditches along the sides of the narrow roads were filled with bright purple heather.

We drove by tiny hamlets, most with only a few stone houses nestled close to one another in close proximity to a church, a grocery store that also doubled as the local post office, and a pub, the center of British social life and conviviality. The walls of most of the buildings were white stone and on the top of each one stood a row of chimneys pots, some with tendrils of gray peat smoke rising into the air and letting us know that the inhabitants were probably home.

After a restful night's sleep at a comfortable bed-and-breakfast across the street from the Dumfries railroad station, we drove two miles west to Terregles, where we hoped to find the graves of our ancestors.

Luck often plays a large part in the success of genealogy searches. It was luck that cousin Olivia Doner told me where to find the Terregles cemetery. It was luck that I found Historian James Corrie and that he, in turn, led me to Jessie Corrie and her map. It was an amazing stroke of luck that appeared in the form of the first man we saw when Jeff, Bob and I drove into the tiny village of Terregles on a bright sunny early fall morning. Bob stopped our car and rolled down the window. "We are visitors from America," I began. "Do you know anything about a family named Corrie who lived in this area many years ago?"

"Oh, yes," he responded with a knowing smile. "Go along this road for a mile. On your right is the farm known as Clunie. That's where the Corries lived."

I was astonished! I had no idea that the land of these early Corrie ancestors including the great-great-grandfather of my William were still identifiable to locals. Then the gentleman added. "You should see Mrs. Parker. She's our town historian."

We followed his directions to the farm known as Clunie and came to rolling fields with a small stone cottage snuggled against a sheltering

Road past the farm known as Clunie.

Stone house at Clunie, near Terregles, Scotland.

hill. The house had solar windows (obviously a contemporary addition), but the aging stones that made up the walls of the remainder of
the building could well go back to the 1600s when William Corrie of
Clunie (he would become the great-great-grandfather of my own great-
great-grandfather William) rented the farm and lived in this home.

The tranquil scene indicated a quiet life for those who loved and
married and bore offspring on this land. John and Alexander Corrie,
William of Clunie's children, were born here. They, no doubt, ran
and played across the undulating hills and down into the valleys and
were probably told, at an early age, that the rounded hollows in the
land are called "corries."

The boys would have helped their father feed livestock, milk cows,
and clean out the barns. As with most children of that period, they
probably assisted in doing the work their mother assigned them such
as gathering eggs, pulling buckets up from the well, and carrying the
water indoors for household use. Every day they would have brought
in kindling and peat as fuel for cooking and heating.

The gentle country landscape seemed peaceful to us, but by the time John and Alexander were grown and had their own families, angry words were being heard on the farm and in the village of Terregles. A disagreement between owner and renter became so great that a grandson of William of Clunie, John's son Adam, lost the farm.

I discovered this story from Mrs. Parker when my two sons and I visited her that day in Terregles. Mrs. Parker told us about the early Corries and their feud with the Maxwells who owned much of the land around the town, including Clunie Farm. The Maxwells were devout Catholics. About 1580, Lord Maxwell rebuilt the Terregles church, originally erected in the 1100s. His purpose was to prepare a

place where he and his family could practice their faith. For a chapel and a burial place for his family, he added a "queir" (pronounced "choir") to the east end of the building. He and his descendants worshipped in that section of the church.

When the Protestant Reformation came to Britain in the 1600s it caused all sorts of problems between the Maxwells and the Corries. And herein lies the story about the first Adam Corrie.

Adam Corrie, William of Clunie's grandson, born 1703, was living at Clunie about 1745 at a time Scotland was not yet over its Catholic—Protestant divisions. According to the church history booklet given to

Entrance gate to Terregles cemetery and two-part church. Church of Scotland entrance directly ahead with oldest Corrie graves at the corner of the building.

me by Mrs. Parker, "When a minister for the Church of Scotland vacancy took place in the Terregles parish, William Maxwell and the Roman Catholic aristocracy plotted to choose a priest after their own views and bring the entire building—now half Catholic and half Protestant—and the parish back into the Catholic fold.

"Adam Corrie, by now a strong Protestant, opposed the Catholic connection, and offered an *obstinate* resistance to their nominee."

"I understand that Adam was considered the heart and soul of the opposition," Mrs. Parker explained. "The Maxwells tried to win Adam to their side by offering him three nineteen-year leases on the Clunie farm. That would be 57 years at a nominal rent, but Adam could not be bribed. He carried the matter before the Presbytery and gained the case and the active part of the church remained firmly with the church of Scotland. But in winning his religious battle, unfortunately he lost his farm.

"The church still stands half Catholic and half Protestant, "Mrs. Parker explained, pulling a key out of her pocket. "Would you like to go inside?"

Terreles church and graveyard. The section of the building on the left is Catholic, and that on the right is Protestant.

"Oh my, yes, of course," I answered, delighted with our continued good fortune.

My sons and I followed Mrs. Parker past the graveyard which held the remains of so many Corrie ancestors and walked into the Church of Scotland side of the church building.

The Protestant sanctuary was wonderfully preserved, and we delighted in seeing the plain pulpit and altar rail, a neat balcony at the rear, and rows of well-worn wooden pews. White metal drip pans were fastened at the end of each pew near the floor to hold worshippers' umbrellas, a nod to frequent rains. The pans were a simple and effective way to collect water. I didn't think to check to see how the umbrella handles stayed upright. Something must have kept them standing.

I looked over the simple interior and tried to imagine an earlier time when William of Clunie might have been married here and later brought his sons to be baptized. Was he carried here himself for a memorial service after his death in the early 1700s? How many of

Interior of the Protestant side of the Terregles church. Left to right: Bob Birkby, Mrs. Parker and Evelyn.

my relatives might have been baptized, married, and eulogized within these walls?

Mrs. Parker guided us to the Catholic side of the church by taking us out through a side door and then into the small entrance to the section prepared by the Maxwell family. It was ornate in contrast to the Protestant side. Candles in sconces on the wall are the only means of illuminating the room except for sunlight coming through the stained-glass windows. Arranged on each side of a center stairwell, wooden pews faced a marble altar and cross positioned under the main window.

A life-sized marble statue of an angel stood guard over a marble railing around three sides of the stone steps that descend into the crypt. I walked quietly down the steps to read the names on the memorial plaques on the wall, all Maxwell kin. Bob and Jeff did not find the dark place appealing and quickly returned upstairs to the chapel. I soon followed them up the steps, out the door, and into the welcoming sunshine.

Interior of the Catholic side of the Terregles church.

Outside the entrance we stood for a moment to take in the old churchyard. It was surrounded by an ancient rock wall with green ivy growing in wild profusion over the stones. A stile of stone steps lifted over one side and down the other. Mrs. Parker told us that the small square stone building near the entrance gate had been the first school in the district, built in the 1600s when the government decreed that every church parish should have a school. I wondered if William of

Two-part church in Terregles' cemetery. To the right is the Catholic chapel and to the left is the Protestant church of Scotland.

Clunie's sons, John and Alexander Corrie, had attended, and later, his grandson, John's son "Obstinate" Adam. Unfortunately, I found no records to answer my questions, but the school's stones seemed similar to those found in the walls of the house and buildings at Clunie.

We turned our attention to the graves themselves. With Jessie's map in hand we had little trouble finding the burial places we were looking for. Located next to the doorway at the Protestant end of the church was the memorial stone of William of Clunie, who died sometime between 1700 and 1717. Near his grave were those of his sons John, who died in 1712 at age 49, and Alexander, who died in 1728 at age 56. A number of their children were also buried in the same plots.

Oh, and we found much more, including the grave of Margaret Halbertson who died in 1774 at 69, and her husband Adam Corrie, who had feuded with the Maxwells about the Church of Scotland matter and who I have come to call "Obstinate" Adam. He died in 1786 at the age of 83. Several of his children are buried beside him.

Jeff and Bob Birkby at the Terregles' graves of William of Clunie, his two sons, John and Alexander, and several of their children.

I left the church and burial grounds with a last poignant look at the graves, feeling amazingly close to all these people. I had learned enough from Mrs. Parker and the man by the side of the road to make our ancestors become real human beings, not just numbers and dates in a genealogy record.

Of course not all of my Scottish ancestors were buried at Terregles. "Obstinate" Adam's two sons, William (whom I call "Uncle" William) and John (who became "Father" John) were not there. I needed to find them, for both were major players in our family history.

It dawned on me that I needed to return to South Park and Borgue to see if another visit would answer any of my questions.

Orange Marmalade

Orange Marmalade is one of the traditional sweets served with scones and crumpets for British teas. The story is that it originated when a ship carrying a load of oranges from Seville was grounded near a Scottish village. One of the residents took some of the oranges home to his wife and she discovered they were much too sour for her liking. Like the thrifty Scot that she was, she found a way to use the fruits by adding sugar, cooking them, and making the first (as far as anyone knows) Orange Marmalade.

6 *large oranges*   4 *cups water*
2 *lemons*   5 *cups sugar*

Peel the oranges and lemons and cut the peel into very thin slices. Cut up the orange pulp. Slice the lemons very thin. Remove any seeds. Combine the fruit and peel in a large pot and add the water. Bring to a boil and simmer, uncovered, for about 10 minutes, then let stand overnight in a cool place.

Bring to a boil again and cook rapidly until the peel is tender. Measure the fruit and liquid. For each cup of this un-drained fruit mixture, add 3/4 cup sugar (more or less to your taste—about 5 cups total). Heat until the sugar is dissolved, stirring constantly, then cook rapidly until the jellying point is reached—about 30 minutes, stirring occasionally. Marmalade will sheet from a spoon when done. Or put a spoonful in a saucer and refrigerate until cool to test the thickness, for it thickens as it cools. Pour hot into sterilized jars and seal.

Genealogy Tip 7: Luck and Persistence

So much of success in genealogy research depends on luck and persistence—finding the right person or persons who can give you a lead—then using one's own patience and grit to follow that lead in the ongoing effort to locate your ancestors.

Don't be afraid to ask for help. If we hadn't stopped a man on the road and asked if he knew anything about a family named Corrie, we would not have found the Clunie farm. If we hadn't searched out Mrs. Parker, we would not have gotten inside the unique two-part church or learned about its fascinating history and connection with the Corrie family.

When gathering information on places and people, and when collecting several family stories, the importance of members of a family sharing information cannot be overemphasized. Cousin Olivia first told me about the Terregles churchyard near Dumfries and a visit she made there. The family history was not complete enough at that time for Olivia to know who lived in the area or who was buried in the church-yard. She was so close! But she passed along the location of the village and some of the Corrie names she found on the tombstones so that I was able to carry the research forward.

Cemetery records can be important. The one I had on Terregles from Jessie Corrie's book was invaluable. By the time my sons and I got to the cemetery, the words on the early Corrie's stones were all but obliterated with moss or worn nearly away by the harsh sea-blown weather. Fortu-nately, we had Jessie's drawing of those stones to guide us.

Trying to read the lettering on worn stones can be a challenge. Some try rubbing the letters with white chalk or flour. Others try doing tombstone rubbings with rubbing paper and charcoal or soft lead.

Church history books, parish records, and local historians can offer family histories and other material that give background stories, such as the one Mrs. Parker gave me.

"May I give you something for your time and effort? I so much appreciate what you have done for us," I said to Mrs. Parker as I turned to leave.

"Oh, no. I like to share the history of this place with anyone who is interested. I don't want anything."

"Then let me give you an offering that you can pass along to the church or use in some way for its work." She smiled and gratefully accepted my gift.

8. The Marble Bowl

In all of us there is a hunger, marrow-deep, to know our heritage—to know who we are and where we have come from. Without this enriching knowledge, there is a hollow yearning. No matter what our attainments in life, there is still a vacuum. An emptiness. And the most disquieting loneliness.

—Alex Haley

Leaving the cemetery of Terregles behind us, Bob, Jeff, and I drove toward South Park. One of my goals in revisiting this place was to find out about an antique black marble bowl that was mentioned in one of the old Corrie family letters cousin Miriam Corrie had carefully preserved. The Corrie family had owned the bowl for generations. Where, I wondered, was that bowl? It made me think as well of the word "corrie" which means a *bowl*-shaped depression. Our name and the bowl seemed to be important in my search for my ancestor William. Could I find the bowl? Would it tell me anything I didn't already know?

Because the road south of Dumfries took us near the home of Margaret Brown and her family, I had contacted these friends from my first trip to the area and they invited us to stop by for lunch. I found myself once more in the village of Castle Douglas at the house called Norwood.

Tom, Margaret and Andrew Brown with Jeff and Bob Birkby.

I had told the boys about Margaret and her husband Tom, about how I met them on my first journey to Scotland, how they welcomed me into their home and then helped me find Historian James Corrie's address. My sons and I got to the Browns' home just in time to gather around the table in the newly remodeled dining area next to the kitchen for a delicious zucchini pie with a cheese topping, crisp fresh vegetables, and hot-from-the-oven cookies for dessert. After a long meal full of good visiting, Margaret and Tom took us for a walk behind the house where we could see the beauty of the countryside with its rolling hills and grazing sheep.

My sons were fascinated by the Browns. "I feel we're friends," Bob said as we bid them good-bye. "I'll be back some day." Jeff nodded in agreement.

South Park was greatly changed since I had first seen it. Thomas Corrie Gillespie, the current owner and the son of Douglas Gillespie, the man I met during my first trip to Scotland, had developed the scenic area into a caravan and leisure park known as "Brighouse Bay

Holiday Park." It had permanent mobile homes people rented for vacation use, lawns where tourists pitched tents, and parking places where families pulled in their recreational vehicles. Thomas had also added a restaurant, lounge, and indoor swimming pool. There are boats, bicycles and riding horses for hire, and a rugged nine-hole golf course. Thomas said he needed the additional income to support the farm and keep it in the family.

A tour guidebook I read called this place "one of Scotland's top environmental Parks set in a quiet, secluded peninsula, with magnifi-

The sign at the entrance to South Park.

cent views over the Irish Sea and is surrounded by 1,200 acres of great walking country. It has everything! you can choose to have a fun filled, action packed family holiday or simply savor the acres of land in this wildlife haven to relax in."

The South Park manor house that William and his two brothers left when they emigrated to America in the early 1800s still stood on the hill. Not far away was the Mill House, used by early owners to grind feed into flour. The rustic stone building, mill wheel still in place, had become a guest house. This delightful lodging, filled, I imagined, with ghosts of my Corrie ancestors, was where my sons and I spent a memorable weekend.

While the boys were carrying the suitcases to an upstairs bedroom of the Mill House, I drank a cup of coffee at the dining room table.

Old Mill House at South Park, now a guest house.

Suddenly, I had the strange feeling that someone was watching me. I whirled around and was startled to come face-to-face with two of Thomas' long-haired, big-horned Highland cattle pressing their noses against the glass.

"Bob, Jeff, we have visitors!" I shouted. The boys clattered down the stairs to join me at the window.

"Look at those horns." Jeff said, raising an eyebrow and tilting his head in my direction. "I hope they're friendly."

"Such cute bangs across their foreheads." I responded. "I've never seen cattle with bangs before."

"Or such long shaggy coats," Jeff said. "It must get cold here in the winter."

Later, when we told Thomas about our encounter he explained, "The cattle fetch a good price at the market but they are even more valuable as an attraction for the tourists. I'm sorry if they frightened you."

"Let's say we found them *very* interesting. I always make a point to prepare for the unexpected, but big-horned cattle staring at me did throw me for a loop." I went to bed that night with visions of my Corrie family tree and of Highland cattle dancing in my head.

The boys and I prepared our breakfast the following morning in the little kitchen of the Mill House, then got ready for the day without a clue as to what we might be seeing. Soon, Thomas knocked at the door with an offer to guide us around the estate. He took us to the barns and buildings built in a square behind South Park house. "Many farm buildings were built in this way in the olden days," Thomas explained, "so the owners could easily care for their animals in the winter. Now I keep my riding horses here for the Leisure Park visitors to ride the trails along the Bay."

Thomas drove us several miles along a narrow country road to the old stone house and dairy farm known as Cairniehill. He directed us behind the house to one of the stone barns. "This was once used to make cheese, but we're no lon-

Bob Birkby stands beside the old mill wheel inside the South Park mill house.

ger in the dairy business. The empty cheese vats are now where I raise my calves.

"Before we go, let me take you in the house. We'll go upstairs and look out toward Brighouse Bay."

I have no idea what the residents of the house thought when Thomas knocked on their back door and asked if he could bring three strangers inside, but they didn't refuse. The lady who answered smiled as she greeted us. Thomas motioned us to the stairs rising steeply from the back door to the second story and led the way into a neat bathroom with a window that looked out over Brighouse Bay and the surrounding land. "Once, everything you see was Corrie land. Over the years, parts were sold. Only Cairniehill and South Park remain."

I wished that the house, the trees, and the land could tell me more of the people from my past. Being inside the old stone house gave me a sense that much had happened there. The broad sweep of Brighouse Bay and the expansive rolling landscape, all part of the original Corrie holdings, made me understand better how my early ancestors must have felt about this beautiful place.

"It's time to visit my father," Thomas said as we drove down the rock-walled lane and away from Cairniehill.

When we pulled up to the front door of South Park, I realized that unlike the leisure park down below, the manor house had changed little since my first visit. Some of the ivy had been trimmed from the walls and a few trees in the windbreak had died and been cut down. Otherwise, it looked almost the same.

Thomas's sister Isabelle greeted us at the door and guided us down the hallway into the living room where her father was waiting for us. Mr. Gillespie was dressed elegantly in a light brown suit and tie. When he motioned for us to sit in the easy chairs by the fireplace, he appeared

South Park manor house. Evelyn and son Bob are to the right of Mr. Gillespie's car.

more fragile and stooped than I remembered. I saw that several pieces of furniture had been added to the room and the space felt more crowded. More pictures of children and grandchildren were on the mantel. Books on an end table beside the sofa appeared well-read. I did not see a television or anything that broke the spell of timelessness.

Isabelle served us a pot of hot tea and lightly-browned scones warm from the oven, along with a cut-glass dish of golden orange marmalade.

"We've wanted to meet you ever since Mother told us about her trip to South Park ten years ago," Jeff began.

Mr. Gillespie smiled. "It was good of her to return and bring the two of you along. What you do back in the States?"

Bob told him about his work writing for the Boy Scouts of America, and about his wilderness work programs with the Student Conservation Association. Jeff explained that he was in conservation and sustainable communities work with the National Center of Appropriate Technology. Mr. Gillespie seemed pleased. "We have done a lot to preserve the land here at South Park, I am happy you are both doing what you are doing."

The boys asked our host about his children. "Well, you know Thomas here. He needs to stay and keep South Park in the family. His daughter Sally is a journalist who gave up her job to travel. At this moment she is bicycling through China. His son Douglas James Corrie Gillespie is a surveyor but is currently a skipper of a tour boat taking charter trips from Norway to the Arctic circle. We keep hoping he'll come back to stay and help. Thomas's third child Julia, is a professional artist who loves to travel. Isabelle is not well and stays here to help take care of me and I help take care of her." Douglas paused and enjoyed a bite of his scone. "I also have a daughter Hannah who is a musician in London."

We thanked Mr. Gillespie for sharing. I was impressed with the variety of talent and interests of his children, although I wondered if any of them would return to Brighouse Bay and South Park to live.

The talk turned to the stock market and the family's interest in homeopathic medicine, then after a second cup of tea and a second scone I felt it was time to ask. "Do you know about a black marble bowl that has been in the family for many years? I read about it in an old Corrie letter."

Douglas put his hands on the arms of his chair and slowly pushed himself up onto his feet. He walked gingerly across the room and disappeared into the hallway. When he returned he had in his hand a large black bowl with a chip out of one side. It looked to me old and worn enough to go back at least to the 1770s when Father John Corrie, the son of Obstinate Adam, was the first Corrie to live in South Park.

Isabelle Gillespie and Bob Birkby admire the family heirloom, the black marble bowl.

"Why are we impressed?" Jeff asked me as he took the bowl and examined it.

"I have no idea," I laughed. "Hold it, think of your ancestors, and fill the bowl with your thoughts."

Bob and Jeff took turns holding the bowl while I took their pictures. They tried to look as if they were considering the meaning of this ancient possession that went back far enough that no one today knows where it came from. When they handed the bowl to me I felt as though I was touching my ancestors, and a chill went down my spine. How had they used it? How had it come to stay in this house and how had it survived so many years with only a chip missing?

I gave the bowl back to Isabelle. As I watched how carefully she handled it, I realized that she treasured it as much as I imagined our ancestors had through the centuries. I knew it was in good hands.

We enjoyed a meal in the Leisure Park restaurant that evening, then Jeff, Bob, and I returned to the Mill House under a sky sprinkled with brilliant stars. When I got up the next morning I looked out of the Mill House windows and discovered that fog had crept in from Brighouse Bay and the Irish Sea beyond, enveloping the land around the Mill House. Its soft white folds made me feel as if the world had disappeared and only this house and those who had lived here remained. The fog embraced us as my mind went back to the late 1700s when Uncle William had purchased the land and left it to his nephew Adam, who had lived here for a time, as did Father John and his family, including my ancestor William. The fog seemed to be telling me that it wanted us to stay. Leaving was almost more than I could bear.

By the time my sons had come downstairs, the fog was lifting and so were my spirits. I got out the book with stories of South Park I had brought with me, and, over breakfast, I read aloud a passage written more than a hundred years earlier by Agnes McNish, a great-granddaughter of Father John Corrie who had lived here for a time.

South Park farm stretches down to the sea. The house is a well-built mansion-like residence in a belt of ash, elm, and oak trees . . . stepping outside of it, and looking seaward, the Isle of Man, thirty miles off, is quite visible . . .

The walk along the South Park shore is full of interest. Huge frowning cliffs throw back the wild waves, and a steady head is needed to walk along the top

Jeff Birkby admires the view of Brighouse Bay from the shore of South Park, Corrie-Gillespie land.

of the cliffs, or to look down and watch the sea playing around their sides. The top of the cliffs is a perfect study for the botanist. Fine grasses and wild flowers of many hues grow in abundance.

When I finished, my sons did just what I hoped they would. They took a walk along the top of the cliffs to *look down and watch the sea playing along their sides.* They snapped pictures of the sea and the view toward the Isle of Man, and brought back grasses, heather and prairie flowers they had gathered from near the Bay. Jeff, botanist that he is, told me that he had found flowers and grasses enough to satisfy his curiosity about the native plants of the area.

We said our good-byes to Thomas Corrie Gillespie and drove along the narrow road that ran past the Mill House, past the RV park, past the drive that curved up to South Park manor house. As we drove past Cairniehill we once more to saw its rock fences, its lush pastures dotted with hillocks, and its calves and cows. We continued past Senwick, which had once been part of the Corrie lands. I watched out the back window of the car until the scene was snatched from my view by a turn in the road.

As the car carried me away, my heart overflowed. I would always cherish every moment of our visit to South Park, but most especially the time I held the black marble bowl filled to its brim with my heritage.

Bob and Evelyn Birkby pretend to be "Elderly people crossing" in front of a sign on the road near South Park and Senwick. And why, Bob wondered, should we beware of the old folks? Will they beat you with a stick?

Scottish Scones

The British have made their high teas into relaxing social events. During the many high teas I enjoyed, I discovered my favorite food was scones layered with strawberry jam or orange marmalade and topped with clotted cream or whipped cream.

2 cups sifted flour
2 Tablespoons sugar
2 Tablespoons baking powder
1/2 teaspoon salt

1/2 teaspoon soda
1/2 cup vegetable shortening
(like Crisco)
3/4 cup buttermilk

Combine dry ingredients in a bowl. Cut in cold, firm shortening until mixture looks like cornmeal. Add buttermilk and stir with a fork just until dry ingredients are moistened and dough holds together. Knead lightly a few times to smooth. Roll out to 1/2 inch thick. Cut into 1 1/2 inch rounds and place on ungreased cookie sheet about 1 inch apart. Brush tops with milk or cream. Bake in preheated oven at 400 degrees for 12 to 15 minutes or until golden brown on top.

Make-Believe Clotted Cream

Real clotted cream is a thick, rich cream with a delightful flavor made by heating unpasteurized milk until a thick layer rises to the top. The milk is cooled and the cream is skimmed off. Clotted cream's sweet flavor makes it perfect to put on scones. Since the real thing is not always easy to find, this recipe is a simple-to-prepare substitute.

8 ounces softened cream cheese
2 Tablespoons powdered sugar
1/2 cup sour cream

Soften cream cheese to room temperature. Stir together with sugar. Fold in sour cream to blend. Keep refrigerated until time to serve.

Genealogy Tip 8: Value of Memorabilia

How can objects like a black marble bowl help us connect with our ancestors? A shiny bodice pin, a delicate hair wreath, a pocket watch, a hand-knit shawl—objects can tell a story about those whose lives we are researching. We do that with our imagination, combining ideas of what might have been with what we know for certain of people from our past. Each item can trigger a story that will be told and retold as you learn of the individuals behind the object. It can carry you back through time.

Things that are passed down to us might require careful care. A wedding dress or an old quilt, for example, should be wrapped in archival tissue paper or unbleached muslin and stored in a special archival box. A piece of a special garment or a tiny baptismal dress can be framed behind glass. If you hang up such a keepsake, keep it out of the light as much as possible. Both sunlight and artificial light can cause fabrics to fade and eventually destroy them.

Family Bibles frequently hold notes helpful in family research. Double-check the date and spellings, however, for handwriting can sometimes be difficult to decipher and the dates don't always coincide with birth certificates or baptismal records.

Learning to care for antiques, fragile papers and fabrics is important. Using acid free paper in scrapbooks, computer printouts, and boxes is essential to long-term preservation. Ask your local library or historical museum for information on catalogues or shops where you can order materials that are archival safe.

9. Relatives Who Stayed in Scotland

We are all on a wilderness journey; may we all be directed by Infinite Wisdom which cannot err in the good "ould" way . . .

—Father John Corrie

The tiny town of Borgue near South Park is a quaint village with a row of charming cottages that give a glimpse into what the place might have looked like when it was a thriving community. In earlier days it was bustling with activity with a school, stores, post office, and an active population that served the surrounding countryside. Its location close to the Corrie lands meant that my relatives were familiar with this place and knew those who lived and worked here. The Corries attended its school and church and, eventually, some who stayed in the area died and were buried in its simple cemetery.

After our stay in the Mill House at South Park, Bob drove Jeff and me to Borgue and parked our rented car near the locked gate behind the village church. The stone wall reminded me of the one surrounding the graveyard we had visited in Terregles. Bob pointed out the stone steps that gave us access to the space inside the wall's confines.

One at a time we went over the stile. We found the graveyard serene and quiet and the church, gray with age, topped by a square Norman tower. I led my sons to the painted memorial that Mr. McMinn had pointed out to me during my first visit here.

"This is the only family burial place I saw on my first trip," I explained. "But the early histories indicate a number of Corries are here. How I wish we had a map of the locations like the one Jessie Corrie did for the Terregles' graves."

A few minutes later, while I was still examining the painted marker, Jeff called, "Mom, come here. This marker says William Corrie— died 1811."

I whooped with joy, too loudly, I fear, for the folks buried in this ancient place. I could almost hear them stirring below us in their earthen beds. This had to be Uncle William who made his fortune in the lace business and who, in 1778, purchased the estate on Brighouse Bay near Borgue that included South Park.

The grave, surprisingly close to the painted marker (which made me wonder why I had not found it earlier), was surrounded by a weathered, waist-high rock wall topped with an ornate wrought-iron fence. An opening at one side gave us access to the interior. Opposite this entrance, a rock wall was built up to the height of the iron fence. It held a rectangular marker on the left side, and there was a space on the right where an oval plaque had been affixed. The plaque was leaning against the rocks at the base. The words were worn and hard to read, but Jeff made them out and said, "Mom, you're right, this has to be Uncle William. It says *Erected by his daughter Jane*."

I looked to see who else was buried in this plot. Among them was Brother Adam's son John (always known as JNO) who had traveled to America to buy the Illinois land for his father. "An interesting

Jeff Birkby stands next to Uncle William Corrie's marker in the Borgue cemetery. The marker on the left is for Uncle William's nephew and Brother Adam's son, JNO.

pairing," I said. "We have Uncle William and his grandnephew buried side by side near the ancestral lands."

I stood still for a time thinking of these two extremely important people in my history, then I went over to examine two memorials in the shape of tables, a type of monument I had seen in other British cemeteries. I let out a second whoop. "I found Father John and his wife Margaret!" As I began to make notes of the names and dates etched into one of the table-shaped monuments, I realized that I was putting together the information I needed to make the picture of Father John and his wife more complete.

I quickly verified that Father John was born in 1739, the fifth child of "Obstinate" Adam. I already knew that Father John was baptized in Terregles, no doubt in the parish church that was half Church of Scotland and half Catholic. He lived part of his childhood on the farm known as Clunie. When his family was banished due to his father's disagreement with the owners, he moved to a farm known as Mallaby where he grew up to become a farmer for a time before moving to South Park.

I also knew that Father John was married in 1765 to Margaret Thomson. (Oh my, another Margaret!) They had seven children, none of whom died in childhood, an amazing feat at the time. Despite being handicapped with severe arthritis, Margaret raised all of her children to adulthood.

According to one of the old letters, Father John's Margaret *was such a martyr to rheumatism that she had to lift the baby from the cradle with her teeth because her arms were so powerless.* The marker verified that Margaret died in South Park in 1812 at age 72 before three of her sons and their families left for America. My mind whirled as I thought of the old letter from Father John I had read in Miriam Corrie's collection in which he wrote about his religious bent, his concern for his three sons in America, and news of the members of the family who had stayed behind in the Scotland.

As I stood at his grave, I imagined that I could hear Father John's voice from another letter he wrote to his son Robert and his wife Sarah in December of 1814. The two were in Dublin at the time. *Do you plan to stay there in the lace trade?* the letter reads. *Markets here are very low . . . it is not possible the farmers can stand long unless a change comes soon.* In just those sentences we see how, as early as 1814, the economy was becoming a concern to the Corries.

Father John included scripture in his letters. At a time when life was fragile, many people depended upon faith in God for solace and strength. In his letter to Robert Father John says, . . . *blessed be to God who, out of loving kindness brought both to you and your partner has restored you to health again. Whom the Lord loveth he chasteneth and scourgeth every*

Evelyn copies data off the Corrie table top memorials with the Borgue church in the background.

son and daughter he receiveth. Resignation and submission to the will of our Heavenly Father is what he expects from all his children. He has promised he will never leave them nor forsake them who put their trust in him . . . .

Father John concluded by saying, *I have settled my worldly affairs and I am resigned to the will of God. If I should never see you or the rest of my absent friends here, may it be our happiness to meet at our blessed Lord's right hand never to part.* He wrote this in 1814, fifteen years before his death.

As I searched on the stone for the date of Father John's death, I remembered a letter written in 1829 by Father John's lace-merchant son Adam Corrie of Wellingborough to his brother Robert in Illinois that tells of their father's passing:

I am sorry to tell you of the removal by death of our beloved and venerable parent on the 23rd December on the verge of his 90th birthday. His daughter–your sister Margaret–was with him frequently and saw him though the whole of his last illness–indeed he has not wanted for anything. I told her that I would see to everything paid which I have done, including all the charges of his funeral, which was reputably conducted. It was attended by all the decent people in the parish. His remains were deposited in the same grave (in the Borgue Cemetery) which contains the ashes of our beloved and most affectionate mother. Peace to their memory.

Oh, what I wouldn't give to know who all those "decent" people in the community were who came to the "reputably conducted" funeral!

I remembered reading that Father John's assets were divided among his children, which surely helped the folks in America immensely.

I began examining the table-shaped grave marker located next to Father John's and his wife Margaret's. It marked the grave of Father John's son, James, his wife and some of their children. The lettering told me that Brother James had married Margaret Affleck. (Yet another Margaret!)

Evelyn stands beside Father John and his wife Margaret's tabletop memorial. In the rear is the iron fence that encloses the space holding Uncle William and his nephew JNO's graves.

Soon I was writing names and dates in my notebook as fast as my hand could function. That stone was a treasure from which I learned that Margaret Affleck, spouse of James Corrie of South Park, died in 1818. This solved a problem in my genealogy dates.

Some early records had said that Brother James' wife died in 1817, but their youngest child was born in 1818, so that first information could not have been correct. As I wrote down the date 1818 to match the date of Margaret's death etched in the stone, I realized that she probably died in childbirth or soon after, as did so many young women of that time. Her husband died the following year, leaving his young family to be cared for by Father John in South Park.

Another sibling of my ancestor William who stayed in Scotland was his brother Andrew. He was not to be found in the Borgue cemetery, but later I discovered that Bother Andrew left a sparse record of his life. I knew he had worked in the lace trade for a time but did not have the financial success of his Uncle William or his Brother Adam. In the family letters, I learned that he became frail in his later years and dependent on his children.

I have no record of Andrew living in any of the nearby Corrie lands. What little I do know comes from a letter to Robert in America written by their brother Adam in the 1830s: *Your brother Andrew is in Bedford with his son Charles who is a druggist there . . . He talks of going to live in Olney (where he once tried his hand at the lace trade). I think Andrew would be happy as a farmer and should go to America but his wife would never think of it!*

It would seem that Brother Andrew's wife was sick and wouldn't let him emigrate. As her health improved, Andrew's deteriorated, so he stayed in Scotland and England and lived most of the time with his children until his death in 1841. But these statements about his interest in America make me think that Brother Adam encouraged all of his brothers to settle on his land in Illinois.

When I checked on the letters for information about the relatives who stayed behind, I found one from Sister Margaret written Sept. 17, 1835, to her brother Robert in America. In it she mentions the death of their brother William, my lost great-great-grandfather: *I received your kind letter a few days ago. I had just been informed of the melancholy event of our brother's death by Adam whom I sometimes say acts as a kind of cement for keeping our family together. I thank you, dear brother, for renewing a correspondence, which had so long ceased.*

There are now only four of us left. I trust, my dear brother, we shall cling the closer together as our family circle narrows to a close. You were the youngest, William was the eldest, and I am only two years younger than he, so this event (words illegible) to me. I am far from strong. My stomach and quinsy in the throat (are two) of the diseases that afflict me most. In consequence my constitution is much enfeebled, so there are sometimes three, four and sometimes five months or so I do not get out of doors. My daughter Margaret is now the only one of my family who resides with me. I brought up a little granddaughter, Jane Kenny, ever since her mother's death in 1822. Jane was then 2 years old. I have 4 sons left out of 12, and 3 daughters and none died till grown up.

Our dear Brother James' family is still living at South Park—a rather delicate family—with the exception of daughter Penelope who is married to an attorney, McNish and lives at Gatehouse of Fleet.... I amuse myself much in the garden [at Senwick—near South Park] when health and weather permit.

The last of the siblings of my ancestor William that I looked for that day in the Borgue cemetery was this sister Margaret. Sadly, I did not find her grave.

Aerial view of Senwick, final home of Sister Margaret Corrie and sometimes residence of JNO.

In the small Borgue cemetery I had learned much about Father John, his son James, and his family. I added the new information to what I had found at the beginning of my search, the smidgens of their lives in the genealogy book from historian James Corrie, notes in Jessie Corrie's book, and what I had read in the old letters. The Borgue churchyard verified the information to these bits and pieces during this successful and fascinating visit there with my sons.

I climbed slowly back over the cemetery stile knowing that I still needed to learn more about those who remained in Scotland, especially Uncle William whose wealth and love for family helped America become the destination for my own great-great-grandfather William.

Petticoat Tails

Shortbreads come in a variety of shapes—squares, rectangles and triangles. The latter are usually called Petticoat Tails. No matter what the shape, shortbread is a sweet, buttery cookie that makes a fine snack or an addition to morning coffee or afternoon tea.

2 cups butter, softened　　　　*3 cups sifted flour*
1 cup sifted powdered sugar　　*3/4 cup cornstarch*
1 teaspoon almond flavoring　　*Dash of salt*

Combine ingredients use your hands to mix them well. Shape into a ball. Wrap in waxed paper or plastic wrap and chill until firm. Pat dough about 3/4 inch thick in ungreased pie pans. Prick with a fork and bake at 375 degrees for about 5 minutes. Lower temperature to 325 degrees and continue baking about 20 to 30 minutes or until golden but not brown. Cutting into wedges makes them into "petticoat tails." Store in a tightly covered container. These keep well and even improve with age.

Genealogy Tip 9:
What You Can Learn in Cemeteries

You can learn a great deal from cemeteries. Beside helping you find dates and names that are helpful, visiting the graves of relatives can give you a sense of closeness to those long gone.

Before going, try to find as much as you can of the location of family burials. Useful sources for burial names and dates are local historical societies, morticians lists, and city and county recorders. Cemeteries in churchyards are often catalogued in an adjacent church office. See if any of your relatives live nearby who can go with you to help find the graves you are seeking.

Rural cemeteries can sometimes be difficult to find. Members of local historical and genealogy societies often know where such cemeteries are located and the names of those buried there. Don't be afraid to inquire for help. If you get close to where you think an old family burial ground is located, stop at a nearby house, knock on the door, and ask the people who live there if they know anything about the cemetery's location. Most people are delighted to be of assistance.

The way in which the sun shines on a gravestone can make a difference in how easy it is to read lettering. Try viewing stones at different times of day and take the time to photograph them so that you can study the information later.

10. Uncle William and the Industrial Revolution

Genealogists are the only people who think taking a step backwards is progress.

–*Iowa Genealogical Bulletin*

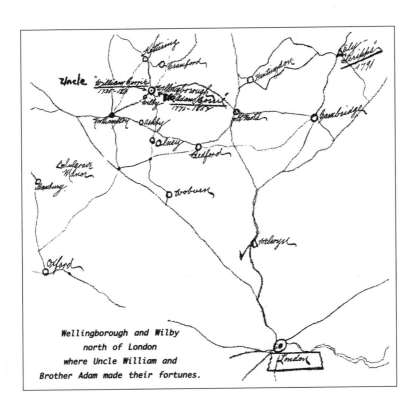

Wellingborough and Wilby
north of London
where Uncle William and
Brother Adam made their fortunes.

When I returned home from Scotland, I spent long hours digesting the sights, the sounds, and the information I had gathered. I thought often of William of Clunie, his eldest son John, and his grandson, "Obstinate" Adam. I checked my genealogy records and added all the information I had gotten from the tombstones in Borgue, and I read and reread the letters written by the relatives in Britain to the immigrant Corries in Illinois.

I realized that two very important people in our family history were two of Obstinate Adam's sons who, in my records, became "Uncle" William (because this William was such a good friend to his brother John's sons and daughter) and "Father" John (the father of the three Corrie brothers who went to America).

Uncle William was born in 1735 and grew up on his father's farm, no doubt learning to work hard, and attending the little school built by the nearby church when the government decreed that every church should have a school. He was the recipient of his father's religious bent and also developed an acute business sense that proved critical to his financial future. When Uncle William became an adult he found himself in the middle of the Industrial Revolution, the perfect man for the moment.

The Industrial Revolution of Britain had actually begun about the time of William's birth. Previously, only very wealthy persons and royalty had been able to possess beautiful frilly laces and delicately woven fabrics, for those had to be created slowly and tediously by hand, mostly by women working in their homes. For generations, an important part of England's economy was based on these cottage industries. The businesses were usually owned and operated by one or more managers who were close to the workers. These men were often known as "bagmen" who would bring the threads and yarns in bags and then put the finished lace and fabrics into the same sacks. The longer it took one person to make a product, the higher the price.

The items were purchased almost exclusive by the wealthy.

According to the *World Book Encyclopedia*, British weaver John Kay invented the flying shuttle in 1739, which cut weaving time in half. His invention paved the way for many other inventions including the spinning jenny and the water-powered frame that made spinning the yarn faster. The cotton gin, the spinning mule, and the power loom were developed in rapid succession, speeding up the process of manufacturing cotton goods and creating a broad market for trade all over Britain.

In the 16th century, lace became increasingly popular in the British Isles. The Corrie family fortunes rose through the trading of Scotch whiskey and Scottish woolens for delicate English lace.

I do not know how or when the Corries first heard of opportunities in the lace trade. It could well have been that the transportation patterns from London north to Glasgow came near enough to Dumfries and Kirkcudbright for the family to learn about this new and burgeoning industry. Information in those days moved by word of mouth and by printed flyers and posters which advertised the need for carriers of lace from England to markets in Scotland.

Andrew, older brother of Uncle William, was the first Corrie to go south from Scotland to Wellingborough, England, and begin selling lace. Uncle William, meanwhile, was developing his own business as a general merchant selling goods that included some manufactured in Glasgow. Uncle William eventually followed his brother to Wellingborough where he established a warehouse and headquarters for his business not far from the lace production center of Nottingham.

I've learned little more about this Andrew, but I do know that Uncle William began to grasp the value of carrying the goods north and then finding products that the English wanted to buy that he could bring back on the return trip. This was not a problem, for he already knew how to obtain these items from his business connections in Scotland.

Uncle William hired men known as "drovers" to do the labor of loading the lace on the backs of mules, then guide the mules north. After the drovers had unloaded the mules, and fed, watered, and rested them, they would load up Scotch whiskey and fine products made from the wool that came from local sheep—sweaters, shawls, blankets and the like. The drovers would bring the caravan of mules back south to Wellingborough.

As historian James Corrie told me during our visit in London, "Scores of carriers were on the road every day carrying Scottish goods to William's warehouse in Wellingborough." William sold the woolen garments and whiskey, bought more lace, and sent it north with his drovers to Glasgow.

James also told me that our mutual ancestor Uncle William had managed to escape a hated tax in Glasgow. "He had his drovers sneak in through the back gates of the city, then, after they loaded up the goods for the return trip, scurry out surreptitiously through the same gates. The drovers also learned the best back roads to take to hide from tax collectors as they went back and forth between London and Glasgow."

Uncle William established himself and his family in the town of Wellingborough, England, and became a very successful businessman. As a result of his knowledge, experience, and hard work, he made a fortune from his ventures. Some family historians list it at £1,000,000, a huge amount even today.

From Jessie Corrie's book I discovered how South Park and surrounding lands came into the Corrie possession. In 1778, Uncle William used some of his fortune to buy the estate in Scotland in the beautiful area on Brighouse Bay near the towns of Borgue and Kirkcudbright. It included the farms of Dunrod Kissocktoun, Senwick, Brighouse, Cairniehill, and South Park. He moved his brother, "Father" John, to South Park.

Uncle William's nephew Adam, son of his brother Father John, must have been a most personable and intelligent young man to attract his Uncle William's attention. This Adam was the next member of the family to go into the lace trade when he joined his uncle in Wellingborough. He learned quickly and began to develop his own business and acquire his own wealth.

Uncle William and his nephew Adam had a good relationship until Adam found a young lady, Penelope Chester Bailey, whom he wanted to marry. Uncle William had a different lady in mind and was so adamant about his choice (the *obstinate* Corrie streak showing up again?) that he told Adam he would cut him out of his will if the young man didn't marry the lady he had picked out. Adam could be obstinate as well. He insisted that no matter what his Uncle did, or how much money he might lose from his actions, he was going to marry Penelope.

And so he did in 1792. His Uncle William made good on his promise and did disown him. Whether the two worked together after that we do not know, but the ironic part of this story comes later. Uncle William died in 1811 at age 76, and was buried in the Borgue churchyard with a memorial marker erected by his daughter Jane. After her father's death, Jane came into his large fortune. Of Jane's four children only one, another William, survived beyond childhood, but he died before his mother.

Uncle William had decreed that if Jane had no living heirs at her death, then his nephew Adam was next in line. Adam had married Penelope and, although he was disowned by his uncle, at his cousin Jane's death he came into Uncle William's fortune. That money was one of the reasons Adam could assist his bothers and sister financially and, eventually, help three of his brothers settle in America. He became the owner of his uncle's lands and houses in Wellingborough, plus the large estate near Kirkcudbright that included South Park, home of Adam's father John.

Now I had a connection with the story Thomas Newton Corrie had told his children around that farm house dinner table in Illinois, and that my father told me years later at ours, about the lovely manor house at South Park. At last I knew how it came into the family and what happened to it when this original Corrie owner passed away.

About 1880, a gentleman in Borgue who knew the Corries wrote: *They were hardworking, industrious kind of folk and kept a hard grip on the tiller but it was generally believed and accounted at once for their success that they had found a pot of gold.* I wonder what Uncle William and his nephew Adam would have said about that—a pot of gold, indeed! It was their hard work and business acumen, besides knowing the best entrances to take their mules into and out of the cities, that helped these Corrie men amass their fortunes.

Trifle

Trifle was probably invented by a thrifty Scot who had left-over cake and custard. It is made with layers of cake such as angel food or pound cake. Layers of custard and jam and/or fruit follow. Some Scots pour whiskey or fruit flavored liquor over the mixture. A pretty bowl or individual goblets makes for a delightful presentation.

Cake layer
Jam and/or fresh fruit
Liquor or rum (optional)

2 cups soft custard
Whipping cream or whipped
topping

Split the cake into thin layers. Put a layer in a deep glass dish or in individual goblets or glasses. Add a layer of fresh fruit and/or jam. Drizzle liquor of your choice over the layers, if desired. Spoon a layer of cooked soft custard (homemade or made from a mix) over all. Continue layering until bowl or glasses are as full as you wish. Refrigerate until time to serve. Before serving, whip cream with a little sugar and vanilla and spread thickly over trifle, or use whipped topping. Sprinkle with a few chopped nuts. Garnish with a Petticoat Tail and a bit of fresh fruit.

Cooked Custard

2 cups milk or half-and-half
3 eggs
Dash of salt

1/3 cup sugar
3 Tablespoons cornstarch
1 teaspoon vanilla flavoring

Combine ingredients over moderate heat and cook, stirring, until mixture coats a spoon. Cool and proceed as directed for trifle. Can be served in sauce dishes for a simple dessert.

Genealogy Tip 10: Sources of Family Records

The story of Uncle William's children is a sad one that was all too familiar in a century where medical care was primitive even in a well-to-do family such as his. This is what I added to my genealogy book about Uncle William's family:

His first child, William, died at age 6. His second son, John, died age 2. His daughter Jane grew to adulthood, married her cousin, Brother Andrew's son Richard Corrie, and had four children, only one of whom grew to adulthood. Next was Margaret who died at age 4, then Mary who died at age 5, and lastly, a son, Adam, who·died at age 18. All his children and his wife Margaret are buried at Cheese Lane Chapel cemetery in Wellingborough. Uncle William was staying at Senwick House on his Dunrod Estate on Brighouse Bay when he died, so he was buried in nearby Borgue cemetery.

In Uncle William's will we see that it was his Nephew Adam who eventually received the bulk of his estate. He also willed money to his other nephews and his niece, giving each of the men £1,000 and his niece £500.

We can learn much from wills. Uncle William's, for example, listed the place where each of Father John's children was living in 1811.

Wills, land records, probate records and the like are valuable for gleaning information about relatives. These are often available in genealogy societies records and in county courthouses. Probate records can include everything needed to settle an estate—lists of immediate family, inventory of property, bills paid, any bills due. Listings of funeral expenses can make for interesting reading.

Obituaries often list survivors and also those who predeceased the person being memorialized. As always, double check the dates and spellings. Like any records, newspapers can have typographical errors.

Church, town and country histories are valuable resources.

11. Brother Adam

And yet, in a larger and truer sense, we are all keepers of the story, for the blood that flows in our veins is the blood of immigrant forebears who sacrificed mightily to carve a new life in a brave, new world.

—*Steven Berntsen*

I t was Brother Adam's fault that my ancestor William got lost. If Adam hadn't made so much money and bought land in America and sent his brothers over to settle it, then his brother William would never have gotten lost in an eastern Illinois farm field and I would not have gone in search of him.

Brother Adam was born in Irongray, Scotland, in 1770, Father John and his wife Margaret's third child and second son. Adam was close to, and became an important part of, his siblings' lives.

From Brother Adam's letters to America I concluded that he was an astute business man with a generous spirit. Adam's thoughtful nature leads me to believe that he was raised in a loving home. It is possible that he was the one Margaret lifted as a baby out of the crib with her teeth because arthritis kept her from using her arms. His familial closeness is indicated by the way he kept in touch with his brothers after they were grown. His letters are very well written, suggesting an above-average education for that period in British history.

By the time Brother Adam was an adult and ready to go out into the world, his Uncle William was well-established in the lace trade in Wellingborough, England, a busy manufacturing town north of London. Adam joined him there. Historian James Corrie told me, "Uncle William gave his nephew Adam £600, a goodly amount of money in those days, to help him start his own business." Adam would have profited from the older man's backing and experience but he had a shrewd head on his shoulders as well; he became successful in his own right.

Adam also had the wisdom to diversify his efforts. Besides working the lace trade, he developed a brick-making establishment, working a clay pit and supplying the bricks to build a gasworks and other commercial and residential buildings. As Adam prospered, he bought land and developed property in the towns of Cheese Lane and Wilby near Wellingborough. Eventually he inherited his Uncle William's fortune and the Dunrod estates on Brighouse Bay that included Cairniehill, Senwick and South Park.

A booklet about Cheese Lane, *Album of the Northhampton Congregational Churches*, says that *Adam Corrie used one of his fields to make red bricks with which he built an estate in northwest Wellingborough.* One hundred and twenty years after the work was done, historian James Corrie walked around the buildings and found them in very good shape. "They looked new without cracks or chips or seemed weather worn—really quality work," he told me.

Adam is described in the Cheese Lane booklet as the founder of the Salem Church in Wellingborough. The Corries had long been members of the Cheese Lane Church but *Adam came out in 1812 as a protest against the introduction in 1811 of an organ into the public services . . . Mr. Adam Corrie led the others to a quiet place beyond the reaches of the organ's distressing tones.* Like his grandfather "Obstinate" Adam of Clunie, who had a disagreement with the Catholics, Brother Adam got into an argument with others in the congregation. When he left the Cheese Lane church in 1812 he helped found a new church which did not have an organ. Ironically, the new church was named *Salem*, which means "peace."

Cheese Lane and Salem churches worked almost independently for some years, but many people were not happy with this arrangement and some services were

Cheese Lane Chapel, built 1746 in Wellingborough, England. Sketch from booklet, A History of Wellingborough, *by Palmer.*

held communally in 1872-1873 (long after Adam's death). Eventually, the two congregations united to become High Street Congregational Church. This combined congregation bought a magnificent organ, part of the cost coming from the sale of the Salem church building. When I read about this event I was certain I could hear Brother Adam protesting from his grave.

Adam's obstinate nature was shown in his altercation with his Uncle about his choice of a wife. Adam had a happy marriage to Penelope, a strong-willed woman as suggested in one of her letters to Sarah Corrie, Brother Robert's wife. "*Never give up your right as a wife to express your own opinions!*" she wrote. (Oh, how I wish I knew what brought on that statement!) Penelope wrote often to the American relatives, and her letters reflect the results of a fine education. In her later years she developed problems with her eyes that made it difficult for her to see. Eventually she became blind and her letters ceased.

Why, with everything else going on in his life, did Brother Adam decide to buy land in America? By 1800 he was no doubt influenced by the shadow of the French Revolution when unrest moved across

Britain. Farm prices dropped and families with many children had a difficult time filling basic needs.

Brother Adam and his wife Penelope had a son John, a lawyer, who always signed his name JNO. JNO played a big role in his father's business. In 1817 Adam decided to send JNO to America to search for a place where he could buy land. In *The Corrie Family Records*, Jessie Corrie states that, "Ever forward looking, it was no doubt in (Brother) Adam's mind that he and the members of his family would then have a safe haven to go to in case times worsened in their home county." Business man that he was, Adam probably thought of this land purchase as an investment as well.

JNO and a lawyer friend, William Gladstone, had a long, hard voyage of thirty-one days over the Atlantic. JNO became so seasick on his return voyage that he never wanted to sail again. No record indicates that JNO's father ever came to America, although one journal of a trip to the States lists an Adam Corrie. I doubt this was our Adam, for ours made no reference to such a journey in any of his letters, and he never seemed to have a real grasp of the situation the new pioneers found upon their arrival.

After arriving in the United States, JNO and his traveling companion went overland to Wheeling, West Virginia, where they embarked on a flat boat on the Ohio River. They floated down to Illinois where they poled their boat up the Wabash River.

They knew about this section of Illinois from the books written in the early 1800s by Morris Birkbeck. In *Letters to Illinois* and *A Journey to America*, he told glowing stories of the Illinois British settlements that were located on the edge of Indian territory. He called the area the "English Prairie" and extolled the values of the land. Birkbeck told of endless supplies of berries, nuts and animals for food, and helping hands among the other settlers. He made it sound as if it would be an easy place to start a new life.

Entries recorded in the *Original Land Entry Book* at the Recorder's Office in the Lawrence County Courthouse in Lawrenceville, Illinois, show JNO purchased land in the name of Adam Corrie in 1818 in Edwards County, (later split into Lawrence and Wabash Counties). John King, a descendant of the Corries, researched in 2001 in the Lawrence County court records and learned that JNO paid $2.00 per acre for his father's land. Records are also in the Vincennes, Indiana, land office. The records of the land purchased by the Corries in Wabash County (part of Edwards County in 1818) were destroyed by fire in the 1850s.

I don't know how JNO carried the $20,000 to the new land to pay for the 10,000 acres he purchased on behalf of his father. He could have had a bank draft to be exchanged for cash at the Vincennes Land Office or the bank of Indiana in Vincennes. Nearby Shawneetown, Illinois, had a bank as well.

When JNO returned to Scotland with deeds for his father's land safely in his pocket, he must have added his own glowing reports to the stories circulating about the new country. Years later in 1898, Jessie Corrie wrote that Adam offered some of this (American) land to each of his brothers and certainly helped finance their emigration and settlement, but did not himself emigrate, his confidence in Britain having been restored. Adam and JNO continued to be farmers on their Scottish lands, either by employing managers or renting out their fields. Eventually JNO went to London to be a general merchant. He found London an unhealthy place in which to live, so he bought property in Windsor, moved there, and commuted to London and Wellingborough only when necessary.

Through the years, Brother Adam wrote many letters to his American relatives, as did his son JNO. The letters from the two give us a broad view of their interest in the fledgling pioneers.

Brother Adam could be stern. He wrote often about his concerns, as in this letter written August 11, 1843: *(I hope) that you will keep a sharp outlook that none of my trees are ever cut down. Do you raise many sheep? What price do you get for the meat and wool? I suppose pigs are a great article of trade with you. We are selling beef at £6 and mutton at £5 1/2. Wheat has been up at late at £1 per bushel . . . Give our love to all the friends in your quarter who are respectable. Indeed, I earnestly hope that they are all so. I hope God's blessing will attend you all for time and eternity.* Adam obviously had no clue how difficult it was to farm land if you couldn't cut down the trees. In any case, he was too late with this cautionary statement, since the trees had already been felled.

Brother Adam's wife Penelope also wrote often to the American relatives. She talked in her letters of sending books to Robert's children. I have the feeling that she also sent books to Agnes, John's daughter, who opened a school soon after her arrival in America, and she probably sent several to Brother William's children as well.

Despite Uncle William's dire predictions, Adam and Penelope had a good long marriage. Penelope died in 1852 and her son JNO wrote about it to the American relatives: *My beloved mother has left us—she is no more. She had been in wonderful good health for her until last Sunday fortnight, the 31st, when she was suddenly seized with paralysis as she was lying upon the sofa at home, during morning service. It deprived her entirely of the use of her left arm, side and leg . . . After languishing a few days in great helplessness, she died at half past 2 in the afternoon of the 12th instant.*

There was, I am grateful to the Giver of all good, much mercy mingled with this, my dear mother's last affliction. First of all, I may mention that although the seizures reduced her to great helplessness of body, yet it pleased God that her mental faculties should be spared and also the power of speech. This gave us all many opportunities of conversing with her about the great things of God and of ascertaining how she felt and thought about Eternity upon which she was soon to enter . . . It was her desire if it might be, to have joy as well as peace in believing . . . There was no distortion of her countenance as is often the case with paralysis . . . When the change came it was without pain and without struggle. She fetched two or three long breaths, her head dropped gently to one side, and she passed. She was in her 81st year and had survived my dear father (Brother Adam) just 6 years and one month.

You will be prepared to learn how beloved and respected she was by all classes in the town as well as by all who knew her who were not of the town. She will be much missed among the poor to whom she was constantly showing kindness.... She was a loving, peacemaking, charitable in the highest sense of the word, meek and humble person . . . Often I have known her to give up her opinions, give up her plans, give up her wishes that other people might carry out theirs.

Penelope, My dear Mother, is to be buried on Tuesday next, the 23rd, when her remains will be deposited in the resting place which already holds those of two of my brothers and my father.

Adam died 12 October 1846, aged 75, in Wellingborough and is buried in the Salem Church precinct. We have no letter regarding his death and can only assume that the letter was lost since JNO wrote in such great detail to his American relatives about his mother's death.

JNO was always involved in his father's business and finally inherited it upon Adam's death at which time JNO divided the American lands among the relatives. JNO also inherited the lands on Brighouse Bay and lived for a time at Senwick. When he died there he was buried in the Borgue cemetery beside his great uncle William.

Painting of Brother Adam's son,
Adam. From Harlan Corrie collection.

Penelope and Brother Adam are buried in the Salem graveyard in Wellingborough next to the church that Adam had founded forty years earlier. Buried alongside them are their five small children and two adult sons.

Adam and Penelope Corrie's memorial
stone, Wellingborough England.
Harlan Corrie collection.

Shepherd's Pie

Shepherd's Pie is a dish served in many places in Britain. Pubs feature it, cooks make it in their homes, and fine restaurants have their own versions they prepare both for tourists and locals.

1 medium onion, diced

1 pound ground beef, or
    leftover roast

2 cups cooked green beans,
    drained

Salt and pepper to taste

1 can tomato soup

2 to 3 cups mashed potatoes

1 egg, beaten

1/2 cup grated cheese

Sauté onion in a little shortening until golden. Add meat and seasonings. Brown. Add beans and soup and spoon into a 1 1/2 quart greased casserole. Combine mashed potatoes, egg and seasonings to taste. Spoon mounds of the potato mixture over top of meat layer. Sprinkle cheese over top. Bake at 350 degrees for 30 minutes. Leftover roast beef is good in this dish. Grind or chop meat into bite-sized pieces and continue preparing as directed.

Genealogy Tip 11: Involving Others

Too often history books neglect important events in the lives of people. Writing our own history, either as children or adults, may be the only way our stories get told. Involving young people, local teachers and historical societies in this kind of an effort will widen the circle of interested people in your community.

Encourage young people in your family, and those in your community, to become interested in their family heritage by helping them look up their family trees and discover any stories and pictures of their ancestors to preserve. Interviews can also be conducted with their own relatives to enrich their knowledge of family. Conducting interviews could be an excellent way for young people to learn about the experiences of those who have lived for a long time, and to help them understand and appreciate the value and contributions of the members of their previous generations.

Talk to the history teachers in your school and ask if they teach local history of any kind in their classes. Do they have any plans when children or young people bring in stories of their ancestors, or do they work through a family tree as a class assignment?

Local groups can do interviews with senior citizens and make audio or videotapes of their stories. Inquire if these local groups are looking for volunteer projects for their school, church, Boy Scouts, or other organizations. Tap into local history or genealogy societies to see if they already have such projects underway.

12. Brother John Comes to America

There are only two lasting bequests we can give our children—one is roots; the other, wings.

—*Anonymous*

By 1818, Brother Adam Corrie owned 10,000 acres of land near the banks of the Wabash River in eastern Illinois, and the idea of settling in America presented a bright opportunity for other Corrie family members. They had a reason to come, the means to make it happen, and land upon which to live once they arrived.

Conditions were hard in Britain. Prices for farm produce were low, crops poor. Other pastures looked greener, and many people wanted to come to America and seek their fortune in the new country.

When Miriam Corrie first read the early family letters she deduced that *"The terrible voyage over the ocean, which was a much greater monster than it is now, the hardships of the raw wilderness, the lack of doctors, of teachers, of preachers, of transportation and communication, what of that? Nothing mattered so much as the lure of that great unknown new land where there was limitless room."*

We do not know what encouragement Adam gave his brothers. It must certainly have been abundant. We know that the family would have had copies of Morris Birkbeck's book *Letters from Illinois* that painted a glowing picture of this new country. These overblown accounts of the wilderness made pioneer life sound far easier than the Corrie brothers and their families found it to be when they arrived, as shown in the following quotes from Birkbeck:

As for what are called the comforts of life, I feel that they are much more easily attainable here than they have ever been to me; and for those who are to succeed me, I look forward with a pleasure which can only be understood by one who has felt the anxieties of an English father.

I have no hesitation in recommending that you do as I have done, that is, to head the tide of emigration and provide for your friends where lands are yet unappropriated . . . suited to my own views, and those of a number of our countrymen who have signified their intentions of following our example, I fixed on this spot in Illinois and am the better pleased with it the more I see of it.

Birkbeck even went so far as to stress the idea that help was near at hand. *As to obtaining laborers, a single settler may get his labour done by the piece on moderate terms . . . not higher than in some parts of England, but if many families settled together, all requiring this article, they must obtain it from elsewhere. Let them import English laborers or make advantageous proposals to such as are continually arriving at the eastern ports.* This no doubt encouraged even more people to come and earn their keep as laborers.

Why John was the first brother to decide to move to Illinois is unknown. He was not the oldest of the brothers. That honor belonged to my great-great-grandfather William. Brother John was born in 1772 in Kirkcudbright, Scotland, the fourth child of Father John and his wife Margaret Thomson. He grew up to marry Mary Agnes Dickson in 1796 in the village of Borgue near his parents' home of South Park, and he became a farmer in a place nearby known as High Banks.

High Banks, the home where Brother John Corrie and his family lived before they left Scotland.

When Brother Adam made the offer to his brothers to go to America and take up residence on the new property, John and his family were the first who decided to go. They spent months preparing for the trip. They stitched their names on every bit of clothing and marked all their household items so they would not be confiscated upon arrival in the United States. In 1819, at age 47, John gathered up his family and sailed from Liverpool.

Mary Agnes and John left two graves in Scotland, one for their eldest son who drowned, and one for an infant daughter. Five children accompanied them to America. After a sea voyage of a month, they landed in the United States and went overland to Pittsburgh, Pennsylvania, where they obtained transportation down the Ohio River. While there, nine-year-old daughter Penelope came down with a fever and died. We have no record of any more children being born to John and Mary Agnes in America.

John brought with him a family Bible (dated 1817) and a writing desk. In Pittsburgh he purchased a cherry chest of drawers and a pilot boat (a flatboat that could hold all their belongings and the family), loaded up their possessions and drifted down the Ohio River to the mouth of the Wabash River. There they poled the pilot boat up the Wabash to Mt. Carmel where they wintered. In the spring, John bought farming equipment and paid $50 to have a log house built, adding another $10 for a chimney and fireplace. With that done, they had a home on their portion of Brother Adam's land in a place they called *Corrieville* (later known as the settlement of *Orio*).

In later years, Ellen Schrader Edmondson, a granddaughter of John and Mary Agnes, wrote to Wallace Beals describing her grandparent's house. *I well remember Grandfather John Corrie's home. It was a story-and-a-half log cabin right on the line between Lawrence and Wabash counties. The house had five rooms below and two small bedrooms above. (Except for the living room) the rooms had no outside doors. One had to go through the living room to get to the bedrooms and only four glass window panes (were in the house), not much fresh air. Our home was nearby.*

Despite all the glowing stories they had heard about the new land, John and his family found their first years in Illinois fraught with hardships. With help, and with funding that probably came from Brother Adam, the work of building a new home was not difficult, but clearing the land and raising the crops was another matter. Farm labor was not as easy to hire as Birkbeck had led them to believe.

The family had to clear the land of oak, elm, hickory, maple, sycamore, ash, and birch. They cut down the trees and then burned them so they could prepare the soil and plant crops. The neighbors came in to help with "log rollings" that some reports say made up piles 10 to 12 feet high which were then burned. During work days, they shared friendly communal feasts.

John and his family, as other pioneer settlers before and after, enjoyed the lovely countryside with plenty of wild plants and animals available for food. Describing some of the beautiful inhabitants, Cousin Dallas Krumm (he of the witching wands) wrote in one of his newspaper columns: *There were insects of beautiful colors and designs in those early days in eastern Illinois. There were many butterflies, moths, dragonflies as well as caterpillars. The rich insect life supported millions of birds. The passenger pigeon made biannual stops in the area. These now-extinct birds were a little larger than a dove. During their migration, they so filled the skies that they blocked out the sun, and several days the light would be like dim twilight or even darkness. This bird was easy to hunt and delicious to eat, so pioneers killed them by the hundreds, dressed them and put them in wooden barrels in layers with salt. They became winter food for hungry families.*

Dallas talks of the many noisy ducks of all sizes and colors that inhabited the land in 1819 and 1820 plus geese, cranes, ibis, mud-hens, and long-legged herons in the river, creeks and marshes. *When they were disturbed, their racket as they took wing was sometimes deafening.* He mentions the frogs that sang in the marshes and streams, and he lists the birds: whip-poor-wills, night hawks, meadowlarks, purple martins, song sparrows, cardinals, bobwhite quail, redwing blackbirds, wild turkeys, and prairie chickens.

The night sounds must have been startling to the newcomers. Dallas wrote that *the howling of prairie wolves (what the pioneers called coyotes), the deeper baying of the black wolves and the hair-raising screams of the bobcat and panther caused a lot of travelers and pioneers to wake and shiver and get out of bed to build up their fires and check their guns and animals. Raccoons, opossum, skunks, weasels, minks, otters and brown bears also were prevalent in the countryside.*

The backwoodsmen hunted bears for their meat, fur and fat. The bears were also a threat as they tended to raid pig pens and also tried to get to the calves and sheep. The black wolf enjoyed what Dallas calls the "barnyard cuisine." Bounties on wolves were levied in eastern Illinois as early as 1816.

Sometimes at night I try to imagine what it must have been like for Brother John and his family to sleep in their hand-hewn beds in that log home in Corrieville. I listen for the sounds Dallas described. Only the baying of a few coyotes hunting in a small pack across the hills near my Iowa home actually come to my ears as I think of all the amazing natural sounds these Corrie ancestors heard so long ago.

Once his house was erected, John built a mill where he ground grain for himself and his neighbors. He also started a post office and created a small store in his home where people could buy necessities.

In due time, the family cleared their land and put in their first crop of wheat. Unlike corn, which could be preserved many months, wheat needed careful storage and rapid delivery to market to avoid deterioration. Broadcast by hand in the fall and tilled in or covered by harrows or drags, wheat was harvested during June or July. The Corries got in their crop as quickly as possible, cutting the stalks with a sickle or scythe, then binding the wheat into bundles and standing them up as shocks for curing and drying. They probably did the threshing by beating the grain out with a flail.

New Orleans was the major market for the people who lived near the rivers. Farmers would float their crops downstream to the city markets. Once they reached their destination and sold their crops, they sold their boats for lumber and then walked home. The journey was long and dangerous. They were often carrying large amounts of cash, and robberies were not uncommon.

Brother John and other farmers in the neighborhood who had wheat built a barge, loaded it with their crops, and started down the Wabash River to make their way via the Ohio and Mississippi rivers to market. The barge was overloaded, due to their lack of experience, perhaps, or the desire to take as much grain as possible in one trip. It hit an underwater snag and it was "stove in." It sank quickly taking all the grain with it—a financial disaster for the new pioneers.

The following winter was severe and John needed further financial help from Brother Adam in Britain to see the family through. With his mill, store and post office, John and Corrieville eventually began to prosper.

Meanwhile, John's daughter Agnes opened a school for the children of the settlers in the log house her father built. Cousin Dallas wrote a description of how he imagined it was for Agnes:

In the 1820's she started a pioneer school in her home near Corrieville. Women teachers were rare in pioneer times, as the firm strength of a school master was often needed to persuade the unruly teenage boys to behave and make an effort to learn instead of just socializing and getting into mischief.

Usually the school term was only a few months in the winter, after the crops were harvested in the fall and before spring planting. Each pupil brought from home what books he could find. Webster's Spelling Book was a favorite and an occasional geography book. Arithmetic was taught by the teacher, usually without the benefit of a text. An English Reader was often used, as was the Bible. Spelling bees were held frequently and were quite popular.

In those times the parents often paid $1 per child to the teacher for the school term of three months. Education was considered a privilege and children eagerly hoped that they could go. Many of the students would walk up to four miles to school over poor roads or a path, in mud, snow, ice and rain to reach the school.

Geese provided quills to make into pens and ink was made from maple bark, sumac and oak galls soaked in vinegar to make a very black ink. The inkstands were often a sawed-off cow horn fitted into a wooden base to form a watertight bottle.

This was the time in the United States when what was called "The Great Awakening" spread across the country. Methodist circuit riders moved through the wilderness bringing religion to the far-flung pioneer families. This was important, for faith continued to be a vital part in the lives of the members of the Corrie families.

Wallace Beals passed along to me several pages from the book, *Highways and Hedges; Fifty Years of Western Methodism*, by John Stewart that mentioned Brother John and his family by name. *In the (Corrieville) neighborhood*, Stewart wrote, *we formed the acquaintance of a Scotch Corrie family, of whom Rev. Beauchamp makes such eloquent mention in his notices of the triumphs of grace in the west . . .*

Methodist Circuit riders ministered to the most remote pioneer families. Engraving of a drawing by A. R. Waud, from Harper's Weekly, October 12, 1867. Copyprint Prints and Photographs Division, Library of Congress.

On Friday we commenced camp meetings . . . The preaching and prayer-meetings were attended with great success and some 45 (persons) professed conversion and 23 joined the church. Of the number that joined is a Scotch family that is deserving of special mention. This family had lately emigrated from Scotland . . . Having none of their own people with whom to associate, they commenced attending services with their neighbors . . . After the meeting they invited me to their home. I accepted and enjoyed further conversation with them.

*Their home and surroundings indicated industry, neatness and thrift, while
the family proved to be intelligent, serious and very hospitable . . . Their education has been such that they have scruples of conscience . . . The family con-
sisted of eight persons: the parents, three daughters, two sons and a nephew.
The family attended the services above described and they were converted as
they bowed at the alter at the same time . . . they all came forward together
and applied for membership.*

*Brother Corrie and his family became, at once, efficient working Christians.
The family was, indeed, a model family and proved to be a valuable acces-
sion to the church.* (I am certain that this happened in the late fall of
1822 or the spring of 1823, for by then William's family would have
been in residence and one of their sons was no doubt the nephew
mentioned in this narrative. I would guess it was William's son Adam,
the one who later married John's daughter Mary.)

Father John in Scotland, who was a staunch (obstinate?) Presbyterian, was shocked that any of his children would leave the Presbyterian
church for what he called the "upstart Methodists." He urged those in
America still faithful to the Church of Scotland to bring the wayfarers
back into the fold.

Soon after their conversion to Methodism, Brother John's family
made the acquaintance of John Scripps, one of the first Methodist
circuit riders to travel extensively in Illinois. He was an intelligent,
good man, and an excellent preacher. When he decided to find a wife
and settle down at the age of 39, he thought of the Corries and their
daughter Agnes. After a very brief courtship, Agnes left her school
teaching and married Scripps. Eventually, they moved to the new
community of Rushville, Illinois, to make their home.

Scripps remained active in community and Methodist church
affairs, and wrote for the local and national newspapers. (The Scripps

newspaper chains, primarily started and continued by members of the Scripps family, came to be known around the country).

Agnes bore seven children and cared for their needs when her husband was away on his religious journeys. It must have often been lonely and difficult for this intelligent, educated Scottish woman.

John Scripps died in 1865 and Agnes in 1866, leaving a Scripps and Corrie legacy in Rushville.

When I first read the story of Agnes marrying John Scripps and moving to Rushville, I realized that this tied in with my visit in 1929 to the Scripps' sisters Henrietta and Eliza. They were descendants of Agnes and John Scripps. I thought of the turret room in their home that held the papers and memorabilia that included records and drawings of the family tree and the story of Agnes and John Scripps.

12 EAST WASHINGTON STREET
CURRENT ADDRESS: 135 EAST WASHINGTON STREET
FORMER HOME OF: REVEREND JOHN SCRIPPS Born 1785 Died 1865
AGNES CORRIE SCRIPPS Born 1800 Died 1866
PRESENT OWNER: TOM AND JIM KERR
POINT OF INTEREST: REVEREND JOHN SCRIPPS IS A DESCENDANT OF
WILLIAM SCRIPPS AND GRACE LOCKE SCRIPPS.

Sign in front of John Scripps and Agnes Corrie Scripps home in Rushville, Illinois. Renfro photo.

239 NORTH JACKSON STREET

FORMER HOME OF: SIX SCRIPPS SISTERS: BEEBEE, MINERVA
HOUSTON, GRACE HEMPHILL, HENRIETTA,
ELIZA AND DELLA

PRESENT OWNER: FORREST AND BONNIE CAIN

POINT OF INTEREST: ORIGINAL HOME, 206 SOUTH JACKSON STREET,
WAS RAZED IN 1990.

Henrietta and Eliza Scripps are the two sisters Evelyn met in Rushville, Illinois, when she was a young child. Renfro photo.

Now, all these years later, I was beginning to fit the pieces of their story together.

Agnes' father, Brother John Corrie, suffered a heart attack and died in his Corrieville home on May 18, 1823, just four years after starting his great American adventure. Members of his family were certain his death was at least partially caused by a broken heart brought on by grief and disappointment in the difficulties he had to face in this new land, including the loss of that first hard-earned crop of wheat.

The entries in the family's expense books following Brother John's death are: *For making a coffin, $1.25; Doctor bill $3.50; Silk dresses $5.00.* (The five dollars was apparently only a partial payment for the silk dresses, for in 1824, 1825 and 1826 more payments were made. I wonder why this listing was plural—*dresses*—and what kind of garments they were.) Recording the will in December 1823 cost $1.75.

A newspaper article from 1876 in the Mt. Carmel, Illinois, *Register* tells of a long-lost burying place: *Reference was made to the old burying grounds in the woods to the east of Mr. John Corrie's residence, and on his farm. It is almost effaced and lost in the long years in which it has been unopened, by the action of the elements and the natural droppings of the forest that has usurped the ground again. This has been hastened, too, by no gravestones at the old graves.*

In that part of the county it seems to have been the custom in those early times for relatives to open a burying place on a farm belonging to some member of the family . . . many have been deserted for one reason on another for many years and the exact location is lost.

On the farm, now owned by E. Kelsy, is a graveyard of some interest. The farm once belonged to John Corrie, Sr., who came from Scotland with a most interesting family and settled there. The household was comprised of the parents, one son Adam and three daughters, Agnes, Margaret and Mary.

It was a rare family to meet in the wild and rough frontier. The ladies had attended school in Kirkcudbright, in Scotland, and were cultivated in their minds and refined in their manners, and were also exquisite housekeepers. Agnes married the Rev. John Scripps, Margaret married Samuel Schrader and Mary married her cousin, Adam Corrie.

This fine old household, this specimen of Scottish piety, wit and taste, transplanted to the wilderness of America, was broken up by the death of the venerated parents. There was a clump of oaks on the slope that lay before their door towards the east, and here, with the leaves of the trees and the "gadding grape vine" whispering above, dewy with nature's teardrops and the untamed vigor of the prairie ground, (the relatives and neighbors) laid the saintly dust.

Here also, in time, other were laid (including William Corrie and his wife Margaret) but now it has long been unused as a place of interment.

This is hallowed ground where the dust of God's children lie sleeping. Alas, how rude and wild a spot received the mortal remains of these genial, devout and well-bred Scottish (persons). No walled church yard with the "bonny heather" growing among the graves, and mournful yews standing guard around an old church, hard by, with storied windows and peeling bells aloft as it was with their ancestors. Instead, they were laid in the midst of the untamed wilderness.

Jesus in glory calls them to behold him and share in the splendors and the solemnities of the amazing scene.

Regardless of the fact that the article said no markers were visible in that farmyard corner, John and Mary Agnes' stone was eventually located, for in 1947 descendants of these first American Corries moved the gravestone and installed it in the cemetery next to the Wabash Presbyterian Church. It was placed not far from where John and his family first settled.

Drying Corn for Food

Corn was a welcome staple in season, and the pioneers learned to preserve it by cutting the cooked kernels from the cob and drying them in the sunshine. Today, the process can be hastened by using an electrically-heated dehydrator made for that purpose, or a slow oven. The dried corn can be reconstituted by soaking it in water or milk then cooking. The drying process yields a delightful caramelized flavor. Current varieties of sweet corn would be different, no doubt better, than the basic field corn grown by the pioneers.

This is my favorite way to cook dried corn.

Creamed Corn (from dried)

1 cup dried corn

2 cups milk

1/2 teaspoon salt

1/4 teaspoon pepper

1 teaspoon sugar

2 Tablespoons butter or
    margarine

Toast or English muffins

In a medium saucepan combine dried corn, milk and seasonings. Let soak until the corn has absorbed at least half the liquid, approximately 4 hours. Add butter or margarine and cook over medium heat until kernels are tender and the corn mixture has thickened—about 10 minutes. Serve over hot buttered toast or English muffins.

Genealogy Tip 12: Sorting a Family Record

As with most genealogists, I sorted each family's records in an orderly fashion. As an example, this is the record of John and Mary Agnes Dickson's family. I use the dates in the manner of genealogists, giving the day, then the month, and lastly the year. This separates the numbers so they can be read correctly.

Brother John Corrie was born in 1772, the fourth child of Father John and his wife Margaret Thomson; John married Mary Agnes Dickson on 5 May 1796 in the village of Borgue near his parent's home of South Park.

John and Margaret Corrie had seven children:

(1) Thomas, born 12 January 1797 in Kirkcudbright—drowned in Scotland.

(2) Margaret, born 8 August 1798 died in infancy.

(3) Agnes, born 1800 in Kirkcudbright came to America where she was a school teacher. Married 1824 to the Rev. John Scripps and moved to Rushville. Had 7 children; died 1866.

(4) Mary, born 1802 in Kirkcudbright, married her cousin Adam Corrie, son of William, (in those days when not many marriageable young people lived near one another it was not unusual for cousins to wed. Descendants are proud to be "double Corries"); died 1887.

(5) John, born 1803 in Kirkcudbright, married 1st Polly Schrader who died in 1845 after the birth of twins, her 9th and 10 children. The boy died, the girl survived. Married secondly, Cynthia Cook.

(6) Margaret, born 30 May 1806 in Kirkcudbright Scotland. (If a family lost a child they would frequently name the next of the same sex by the same name.) Married in Corrieville 22 August 1825 to the Rev. Samuel Schrader. This Margaret rode horseback through the countryside raising money to build a Methodist church which eventually became Bethel.

She had 11 children. The youngest, Ellen, wrote the description of her grandfather John Corrie's log house. (When I was a young girl I knew Ellen as an old, old lady living with her son. Sadly, I had not yet learned to talk to older people about their memories.)

(7) Penelope was born in Kirkcudbright 13 December 1810. Died "of a fever" in Pittsburgh, Pennsylvania, in 1819 during the family's journey to Illinois. My search for her burial place in the two oldest Pittsburgh cemeteries was not successful.

I was delighted to find copies of Birkbeck's books, guided by my cousin Dallas Krumm, who told me that I could purchase copies from University Microfilms, "Books on Demand," Ann Arbor, Michigan. The originals were printed in 1817 and 1818 for Taylor and Hessery, 93, Fleet Street, London. I bought my copies at a hefty price, but I was very pleased to be able to read what my ancestor William and his brothers did before they emigrated.

13. Brother William Comes to America

Lift the wings
That carry me away from here
And fill the sail
That breaks the line to home.
But when I'm miles and miles apart from you
I'm beside you when I think of you
And I'm with you when I dream of you
And a song will bring you near to me.

—Lyrics taken from "Lift the Wings" *

It was a gorgeous sun-filled, blue-sky day that found me sitting on the balcony of my cabin on a paddlewheel boat moving over the waters of the Ohio River. In addition to watching the passing scenery, I was reading books about the river and the pioneers who first floated down this inland highway.

One of the dilemmas I faced as I tried to get my head and heart inside the life of my William was how I could get a feel for the Ohio River down which he and his family journeyed. I needed to travel that river myself. The way I chose was to take the *Mississippi Queen*, one of the steamboats of the Delta line. I asked my husband Robert, my sons Bob, Jeff, and Craig, and Craig's wife Sharon and their son Nick, to come along.

*Written by Bill Whelan ©1994, McGuiness. Used by permission.

The Birkby family as they boarded the Mississippi Queen for the Ohio River trip. Left to Right: Evelyn, Jeff, Bob, Sharon (Craig's wife), Robert, Craig and his and Sharon's son, young Nicholas. Used by permission from the Delta Queen Steamship Co.

I wanted them to understand the experience so many immigrants had in the early part of the 19th century.

One of the books I was reading on the ship's balcony was a reproduction of *The Navigator*. Brother William would have had an early edition of the book in 1822 when he and his family floated down the Ohio on their way to the Corrie lands. It included *terse but trenchant particular directions on how to navigate the Ohio to the immigrants traveling on boats.* It stated that travelers should *Be careful that the boat be a good one for many of the accidents that happen in navigation on the Ohio River are owing to the carelessness or greed of the boat builder putting the lives and properties of a great many people at manifest hazard.*

The Navigator was written by Zadok Cramer in 1808, and was a must read for anyone piloting a craft down the Ohio. Although not a particularly rocky river, it was full of sandbars, islands, blind corners and tricky chutes, channels, and snags. It meandered through horseshoe bends and oxbows. Many travelers struggling with burdensome flatboats relied on the book's charts to see them safely through.

Emigrant family floating down the Ohio River. Courtesy of Heinz Pittsburgh Historical Library.

I studied the directions on how to find the deepest river channel, how to miss the rocks and snags, and where the islands and villages were located. I looked out over that same water, trying to get a sense of how it looked when the Corries floated by. I tried to ignore the modern energy plants, the long coal barges moving up and down the river pushed by tugboats, and the modern locks through which our steamboat passed. Cities including Maysville, Marietta, and Cincinnati had been small villages in the early 1800s.

Cover of The Navigator *reprint.*

Late at night, long after Robert and I had gone to our cabin and to bed, the younger members of our group gathered on Craig's balcony and watched the passing scene. Electric generating plants lining the riverbank sent power across the countryside to keep the lights burning, fuel the manufacturing centers, and aid in transportation. Large cement towers used to dispel extra gases created by the burning coal sent up huge flames that showed like gigantic Fourth of July displays shooting up into the dark night sky. "It was truly amazing," Jeff told us the next morning. "We went to bed late because we didn't want it to be over."

Even with all these noisy, modern intrusions, I could see enough undeveloped land bordering the stream to picture what it looked like long ago. As I watched from the balcony, stood on the prow as we sailed around a graceful bend, and stopped at the historic ports, I added to my knowledge of what it must have been like when William and Margaret floated their flat boat through its waters with daughter Margaret and her new husband, John Milligan. Also on board were William Jr., James, Adam, Andrew, Joseph, Thomas, Jannet, Mary and George, plus all their worldly possessions.

Some areas along the Ohio River look much today as they did when William and his family floated by.

A place of special interest to me was Blennerhassett Island where our paddlewheel ship docked and we went ashore. The guide told us that the huge gum tree near the landing had been standing "for well over 200 years." The tree would have been there when the Corries passed by. They probably tied their boat up for the night and built a fire under this very tree and cooked their evening meal.

"I can see Mary and George running along the bank and playing with children from other families stopping for the night as well," I imagined. "They ran and squealed and threw rocks into the water and patted little shapes with their hands in the mud at the water's edge."

"I want all of you to pose under this old gum tree. Yes, that big one right there. Come and I will take your picture." After I pushed the button on the camera, I struck a formal pose. "I hereby declare that from now on forever more, this gum tree will be known in our family as The Corrie Tree!"

Blennerhassett Island with the huge "Corrie" gum tree from the early 1800s—for it would have been thriving when the Corrie brothers floated by. Left to right: Bob, Nick, Craig, Sharon, Robert and Jeff.

That night in bed in our *Mississippi Queen* cabin Robert and I shared, I thought of William back in Scotland finally deciding to leave the land of his birth. I wish I knew if Margaret had a voice in this plan, or if William, as head of the family, made the arrangements himself. She had to have been a strong, capable woman to keep her active family together, clothed, fed, and comforted, so I hope she had a chance to express her opinion. (I can't help but wonder if she followed the advice of Brother Adam's wife Penelope who wrote to her women relatives *Don't ever give up your right to make your own decisions.*)

As the family prepared to leave Scotland, life would have become even busier for everyone. They would have sewn clothing for each person, planned the food they would need on the ship, and decided what household items and farm equipment would be essential for

The Mississippi Queen paddle boat was enjoyed by the Birkby Family as they reprised the trip their ancestor William took in 1822 on the Ohio River. Robert and Bob Birkby in the foreground.

their new existence. Some of the Corries had servants, and their help would have hurried the process along as they readied for the trip. The relatives, vitally interested in this project, could have helped as well.

We know from the letters JNO Corrie later wrote to his uncle, Brother Robert, as Robert was getting ready to emigrate, that he had some recommendations for his Uncle William's trip as well. As a result, some of the medicines William would have packed were calomel, castor oil, calcined magnesia and laudanum, a popular pain killer of the day that was really an opiate.

JNO added another suggestion, *Don't forget a little good brandy and a little good rum, both of which you will also get at Liverpool of choice quality. Try and see if the captain of the ship can sell you a little of each before you go on board, as these gentry usually bring it with them, and what they have is uncommonly good. Get everything settled with the captain hard and fast before you put a single thing on board* (so as not to be cheated).

JNO gave his uncles one more bit of advice. *A few oranges, a few lemons, and a few sweetmeats on board with you will be found invaluable, and a couple or three pounds laid out on articles at Liverpool, you will not regret. No one can conceive but those who, like myself, have suffered severely from seasickness, how delightfully refreshing the juice of an orange is when you begin to recover from the effects of it.*

William and his family gathered garden seeds, plants and bulbs which were light and not too bulky to bring in case these essentials were not available in Illinois. What farm implements they brought from Scotland or purchased on arrival in the new land are not known.

With so many emigrating during this time, a number of ships were available for the journey. In his book *Notes on a Journey to America*, Birkbeck wrote that the vessel he traveled on was *fitted up commodiously for passengers especially of the steerage class. She was advertised to sail for*

New York and Philadelphia, and printed bills to that effect were distributed. She took in two-hundred passengers at twelve guineas a head, for a berth, fire, and water . . . I have no doubt that the ships the Corries sailed on were much the same.

The family left Scotland immediately following the marriage in Borgue of William and Margaret's eldest daughter Margaret to fellow Scot John Milligan on June 2, 1822. The newlyweds, along with William and Margaret and nine of their children, said their farewells at South Park, including Father John, whom they knew they would never see again, and traveled overland to Liverpool where they boarded their ship and spent four or five weeks on the small vessel. I hope they took with them more than just a few lemons and oranges!

Once in the States they would have followed JNO's advice to go overland via covered wagon. *When you get to the port you sail for,* JNO wrote, *go (inland) by a hired wagon . . . make a bargain as you can with the wagoner to carry you and your luggage there. A few dollars more to enable you to ride will be well laid out rather than walking and being exposed to much heat and fatigue. You will find plenty of covered wagons constantly carrying goods into the interior, and this is the sort of conveyance you should go by.*

There were three principal points of embarkation on the Ohio River: Brownsville (Redstone), Pittsburgh, and Wheeling. The first was closest to the East coast. Wheeling had the disadvantage of being nearly sixty miles farther inland, and it could be difficult to purchase an outfit there. Pittsburgh, at the point where the Monongahela and Alleghany merged to form the Ohio River was, by and large, the best point for departure. Some of the residents rented parts of their homes to immigrant families preparing for the trip down river.

We know that Brother John had wintered in Pittsburgh in 1819, for it was there his youngest daughter had died. Knowing that his brother had left a small grave in the Pittsburgh area would have saddened William and wife Margaret and no doubt made them doubly careful in caring for their own children. In a period of great mortality for children and young adults, it was amazing good fortune that all of William and Margaret's eleven children grew to adulthood.

The bustling town of Pittsburgh must have been exciting for the immigrants as they prepared for the river journey. William's family would have wanted to get everything in readiness for the fall rains which make the river level high enough to carry their craft safely over the rocks and sandbars which the summer's lower water exposed. The rains also lessened the travelers' fear of malaria and cholera.

Did they choose a carpenter to build them a boat or did the family, with its several young, sturdy men, build their own? I wondered about that as our paddlewheel steamboat docked in Pittsburgh.

The first place I wanted to visit in Pittsburgh was the Heinz Regional Historical Center. There I found books describing all kinds of craft used in the early 1800s for the trip down the Ohio: arks, keelboats, scows, flatboats, rafts, canoes, pilot boats, barges, skiffs, and who knows how many hybrids; anything that could float and carry people, provisions, and livestock with no propulsion but gravity.

A family could buy a boat for $35.00 with a shed-like shelter and an open bow for animals. A fireplace cost $10.00 more. If they did not want to spend the extra money, a family could use a simple box on the deck filled with rocks and sand as a base for a fire for cooking and warmth on their journey.

William and Margaret got the family's belongings organized for the trip down river: chests of clothing and dishes, barrels of provisions that they could get in Pittsburgh, and miscellaneous articles for everyday use. They needed to take enough food for the start of the trip—bacon, beans, coffee, flour—plus fishing poles, guns and ammunition to augment their larder with fish and wild game, and firewood to use to prepare their first meals. Later, more kindling would have been available on the tree-lined banks of the river when they stopped at night.

I try to visualize the farming tools William piled in or on top of the storage cabin, and the grain and hay in the middle of the boat. Many of the pioneers took animals to help feed them on the way and to assist in the farming operations once they arrived at their destinations. The animals were confined at the front end of their craft. Caring for the horses, cattle, and poultry gave the younger members of the family important chores to do.

As I read the stories of early travelers, I thought of Brother William arranging for a flatboat to use for the family's river transportation. Time was running out and they needed to get down the river before winter set in, so William probably purchased his flatboat from one of the local shipbuilders. Everyone could then have helped load it. I imagined slowwitted two-year-old George and little five-year-old Mary picking up and carrying on board the wooden trimmings from nearby boat building projects to use as kindling. Finally, William moved the livestock onto the boat—a milk cow, a horse or mule, maybe a dependable ox, several hens and a rooster, two or three pigs and (I hope) a puppy and a kitten as pets for the children.

When they pushed off and floated out into the unknown, all thirteen family members must have felt invigorated and excited. At last they were on the final leg of their long journey. Soon they would step onto the land where most of them spent the rest of their lives.

The flatboat floated slowly down river, giving everyone plenty of time to see the wooded hills sloping down to the shore, and the

Lush vegetaion along the bank of the Ohio River.

lushly vegetated islands. The dense stands along the riverbanks included sycamores, paw paws, cork elms, catalpas, walnut and gum
that gave the scene wonderful splashes of color. Even more was added
by bright blooming flowers and grasses.

I imagined startled ducks and cranes flying off as the boat passed
by. Everyone in the family would have listened closely to the whistle
of the quail, the calls of rose-breasted grosbeaks, and the cheerful
whip-poor-wills. Martins and swallows swooped down around them
catching mosquitoes and other insects. Just as I did, my ancestors
must have seen majestic bald eagles perched on the limbs at the tops
of tall sycamores and kept a lookout for osprey nests.

For fear of running into snags or sandbars in the dark, most of the
early river boaters tied up their crafts at dusk. The flatboat owners
liked to stay close to one another so the men could take turns in
the night guarding against wild animals or thieves. Friendships were
forged, kindnesses exchanged, and the children enjoyed playing together. Hunting parties on the land shot squirrels, rabbits, deer, wild

turkeys, and an occasional bear. Those back at the boats built camp-fires on the shore and had kettles of boiling water ready to make the fresh game into stews or soups when the hunters returned.

Farmers along the way sold their surplus vegetables and fruits to the immigrants, and sometimes the boaters found a mill where they could buy cornmeal or flour to use in baking their quick breads.

By the time the Corries floated down the Ohio, the towns of Marietta, Lawrenceburg, Cincinnati, and Maysville were well-established. Begun in the 1780s, Maysville was one of the most important towns on the river where the travelers could stop to restock groceries for themselves and feed for the animals and to discuss the conditions along the river between there and Cincinnati. In 1822 Maysville had twenty-eight dry goods stores, one large china shop, four groceries, an iron foundry, a paper mill, and a stoneware manufacturer. It also had three thriving churches (Presbyterian, Baptist, and Methodist). I wonder if the family visited the Presbyterian church to see if it was similar to the ones they had left back in Scotland.

I hope that William had as exciting a time on the Ohio River as my family and I did. Every day, the past and present merged as I rode the *Mississippi Queen*. I felt that William and his family were floating right along with us, and that I was on that crowded flatboat with them over 150 years ago.

Simple Corn Bread

Quick bread made from ground corn was often used by the pioneers. It could be mixed quickly, spooned onto the back of a metal shovel and cooked over a campfire on the riverbank. It could be baked by putting the batter into a heavy skillet or Dutch oven, covered with a lid and then put on the fire with hot coals shoveled on top to give the contents heat throughout. Once in their permanent homes, the early settlers would eventually have had stoves with ovens in which cornbread could be baked. The same techniques were used with biscuits made from wheat flour.

1 cup white flour	2 eggs
1 cup corn meal	1 cup milk
4 teaspoons baking powder	3 Tablespoons butter, melted
1/2 cup sugar	

Mix all ingredients together. Put into a greased 8-inch square Pyrex baking dish, or in an ovenproof skillet. Bake at 400 degrees for 30 minutes or until nicely browned on top.

Genealogy Tip 13: Unexpected Sources

Each researcher needs to decide what is important for the use of the time available. For me, walking on the land where my ancestors lived, seeing their homes, and being on the Ohio River down which they traveled were vital to my gaining a sense of closeness to them. I'll never know how accurate my imaginings were, but the journey we took on the Mississippi Queen was exciting and I found it extremely helpful in understanding what William and his family must have experienced.

Background stories can be found in unexpected places—the boat's library was a help as I read the stories of others who had traversed the Ohio's ever-shifting waters.

The Heinz Regional History Center in Pittsburgh held many stories of early immigration experiences. I found enough about the way houseboats were built and the way in which the craftsmen of the area helped travelers to satisfy my curiosity. Finding reprints of old books like "The Navigator" was especially useful. My son Jeff found a copy for me via the internet. The internet is invaluable in present day research for locating all kinds of resources.

14. William Arrives in Illinois

Oh, the moonlight's fair tonight along the Wabash,
From the fields there comes the breath of new mown hay.
Through the sycamores the candle lights are gleaming,
On the banks of the Wabash, far away.

— Lyrics from "On the Banks of the Wabash, Far Away" by Paul Dresser

When Brother William Corrie and his family came to the confluence of the Wabash and Ohio Rivers, they knew they were near the end of their long journey. With stars in their eyes and many dreams they hoped would be fulfilled, they turned their craft north toward Brother Adam's land in Illinois.

Illinois in the early 1800s was at the western edge of what was then the United States, and the land was newly opened for settlement. More of the fertile soil lay farther west, but that was Indian land and not available for purchase. The first English settlers to arrive envisioned a great influx of British immigrants who would make it a little England. Those years were still close enough to the Revolutionary War and the French and Indian Wars for prejudice still to exist toward newcomers.

In 1817 and 1818, when Morris Birkbeck published his books about his journeys to Illinois, he painted a glowing picture of the newly-opened land that lay next to the Wabash River. *Our soil appears to be rich, a fine black mould inclining to sand, from one to four-feet deep, lying on sandstone or clayey loam; so easy of tillage as to reduce the expense of cultivation below that of the land I have been accustomed to in England . . . The rent of a cabin with cow-horse-pig sty, water well, and garden of one acre, with a common meadow and common pasture, equal to two acres in each, will not exceed 20 dollars a year. The tenant keeping the fence of his garden and his buildings in repair.*

Birkbeck continues, *Labor, including that of horses, is somewhat lower than in England . . . 75 cents per day is the wages of a man boarding himself. A man and two horses may be hired to plough at a dollar a day.*

It is not the sort of independence that will excuse you from labor, or afford you many luxuries! When you arrive you will take your leave of dependence on anything earthly but your own exertions.

The Wabash River is 475 miles long and flows from northwest Ohio across northern Indiana, then forms the Illinois-Indiana border before draining into the Ohio River. The name "Wabash" is an English spelling of the French name for the river. For 200 years, from the mid-1600s into the 1800s, the Wabash River was a major trading route linking Canada, Quebec and the Great Lakes to the Mississippi River. It is beautiful, broad, and pleasant enough to make people want to write songs about it. The current could be swift in the middle, but near the shore it was calmer and more conducive to immigrant families poling their flatboats upstream to their destinations.

The Corries might have disembarked at Palmyra, the closest village to their lands, or they could have gone a little farther north to Bonpas Creek, which was wide and deep enough to accommodate their heavily-laden watercraft, and gone to within half a mile of Adam's many acres.

The first thing William Corrie would have done when he landed was send one of his boys to let his brother John know they had arrived. John would have known these relatives were coming, for William could have sent a letter via travelers embarking ahead of him when he first arrived in America, and then another from Pittsburgh.

What a joyous greeting that must have been! William's family would have brought news and letters from Scotland, as well as gifts and perhaps some new farming equipment.

Adam assigned the land where he wanted his brothers to reside, but he gave them the choice of where to build their homes. William and Margaret settled their family just north and a little west of John's land not far from Corrieville. It was called "Decker's Prairie," named after two brothers who had lived there and then moved on. There were several other prairies in the area and their names are descriptive: "Lick Prairie" (so named because of the many salt licks), "Round Prairie" (near Lancaster), and "Barney's Prairie" (near Friendsville).

Since we know that Brother William and his family arrived in the autumn, their first task was to build shelters for themselves and their livestock. Dismantling the flatboat would have been relatively simple, especially with his family and Brother John and his 19-year-old son, John Jr., to help. The horses or mules that William brought from Pittsburg could have pulled the lumber to the building sites.

Most pioneer families of that time constructed a big fireplace at one end of their cabin for heat, cooking, and light. Many lodgings had lofts reached by a ladder. The hams, bacon, *A cabin similar to many poineer homes in the Wabash County area.*

strings of onions, as well as the beds of some of the children were in the loft. Sometimes the buildings were drafty. Snow and rain could blow through the cracks in the walls. Despite such problems, I have a hunch the older sons of Margaret and William used the loft for sleeping, leaving young Jane, Mary, and George to sleep with their parents below.

Window coverings were made from strong paper soaked in raccoon or bear grease to make them transparent enough to let in a little light. The door would have been small, facing south or east (away from the north winds), with leather straps for hinges. A simple wooden latch on the inside of the door with a latchstring was the main lock.

The family had to build a pen for the family horses or mules and the cow that had kept them in milk on their river trip. A cow was a prime necessity for the family, especially with little George and his sister Mary. Milk, butter and cheese were a vital part of their diet. Each spring the family hoped the cow would produce a calf and in the process the cow would "freshen" to continue providing milk.

Another immediate need was a place to house the chickens, ducks, and geese. Any fowl that ran free provided a meal for coyotes or bobcats. The chickens supplied both meat and eggs for the settlers, and the women used the down and feathers for pillows and comforters.

The Corrie men hunted wild game—deer, bear, wild turkey, duck, prairie chicken, quail, and squirrel. The cane brakes along the banks of the rivers were home to raccoon, opossum, skunk, weasel, and mink. Fish swam in the streams. Maple sugar and wild honey were the most common sources of sweetening. There were nuts in abundance. Berries and fruits grew in the wooded areas, and I hope that Margaret and her daughters picked them, dried them in the sunshine, then stored them in the loft to use with winter meals.

At first, the family's staples were what they brought with them or purchased at Brother John's store and mill. Margaret and her daughters made their bread and porridge from ground corn and wheat. Later, the grain they raised in their newly-cleared fields added to their food supply.

The men dug a hole in the ground near the house to make a simple cellar to store potatoes and apples. They lined the deep depression with prairie grasses, added the root vegetables, and fruits, and then covered them with more grass to keep them from freezing.

As soon as winter came, William probably butchered one of the hogs he had brought down river to provide lard for cooking and fat for making soap. They hung the bacon and hams near the fireplace to smoke and dry, then tied them to the rafters of the loft for safekeeping.

The autumn days were busy as William and his family built their home, fenced in their livestock, planned outbuildings for the farmstead, and preserved what food they could. The men also began the arduous task of clearing a field for crops and a garden. The easiest soil to work and the most fertile was near the streams and under the trees, but before it could be cultivated, William, John Milligan, and William's sons had to cut down the trees. If the trees were too large for easy sawing, they stripped off girdles of bark so that by the next year the trees were dead and could be cut down more easily. They chopped off the larger roots near the surface to make it simpler to cultivate the soil.

The initial plowing of newly cleared ground was a difficult task. The farmers plowed back and forth, then cross plowed in the same manner to soften the soil. Blacksmiths were an important part of the economy. They made and repaired the crude plows, and gradually produced newer and better ones.

Corn was one of their staple crops. In the spring, William and his sons planted their first crop by dropping kernels into holes made with an ax or a pointed stick and then covered them with the scrape of a boot heel. "In established cornfields," Morris Birkbeck reported in *Travels in Illinois in 1819*, "yields of that time were from 50 to 80 bushels of corn per acre," but surely he exaggerated that amount as he did with almost everything else! Corn was ground into food or the ears were fed to the animals. Some made it into marketable whiskey.

By the autumn following their arrival William's first crop was ready to harvest. The men husked the ripe corn by hand and tossed it into wagons pulled by horses and oxen. After the corn was picked, he could have turned his hogs into corn fields to "hog down" the stalks and glean missed ears. Many farmers cut and shocked some of the stalks before they were ripe, then later husked the ears and fed the fodder to horses and cattle. Still others picked ears from stalks and piled them in a barn for a husking bee.

I feel certain that the Corries had arrived in Illinois with enough clothing to last them for a time, although the women devoted many hours mending garments to preserve them as long as possible. Eventually they would have spent many evenings at the spinning wheel and working the loom to produce cloth for trousers, shirts, and dresses. The men tanned animal hides and made shoes and moccasins for the family.

Margaret was not only a mother and housekeeper but, as was the case for most pioneer women, she also milked the cows, raised and preserved much of the food, made wool and flax into clothing, administered medicine, and served as midwife. There was no idle season for men, women or children. The day began at sunup and ended at sundown—*from can't see to can't see*, according to Cousin Dallas.

The children did what they could. Most were involved with chores before they reached their teens. In the early census records, by the age of ten many boys were listed as *farmers*.

After washing their clothes along the banks of the Ohio during their journey on the flatboat, the ladies found this task little changed in their new home. They carried clothes to the streams where they built fires, heated water in large kettles, and scrubbed the clothes with homemade soap. The ingredients for soap were readily at hand— bear or hog grease and lye from ashes. They hung the wet clothing outdoors when the weather permitted. If it was raining, they dried the clothing in front of the fireplace.

Everyone quickly realized that they depended upon all the members of the family and their labor for the bulk of life's necessities. As time passed, they produced a surplus of items that could be sold or bartered so that they could expand their homes and possessions.

As time went on, mills, blacksmith shops, a general store, a church, and a school provided the nucleus of a village. In the coming years the sense of community in Corrieville and the Decker Prairie area deepened as younger members of the local families grew up and married. Neighbors helped each other during planting and harvesting, and were there to sustain those close by in times of trouble.

I wish I knew if Brother William's children went to the school taught by their cousin Agnes. If not, they might have been tutored at home. At least we know the family thrived and grew and adapted to their new land.

Margaret died in 1829 at age 54, seven years after her arrival in Illinois. William and their children buried her in the farm field not far from their homestead, close to the same corner where Brother John had been buried a few years earlier. She was survived by William, Jr., then 30, Margaret age 29, James 27, Adam 26, Andrew 23, Joseph 17, Thomas 15, Janet 14, Mary 12, and her youngest son, slow-witted 9-year-old George.

At 70 years of age, thirteen years after coming to America, Brother William died *under mournful circumstances*. (No one today has a clue what that phrase from one of the saved letters means.)

After his death, many of Brother William's belongings were sold. The bill of sale lists buyers and the prices they paid. William's sons Andrew, Adam, and James, and his son-in-law John Milligan, bought a number of the personal items.

A SALE BILL OF THE ESTATE OF WILLIAM CORRIE, LATE OF LAWRENCE COUNTY, DECEASED.

The seventh day of May 1836

Purchaser's Names	Articles	D$/C¢
Andrew Corrie	1 Linen Shirt	.50
Same	2 Flannel Shirts	1.25
John Milligan	1 Vest	2.00
Same	1 pair Britches	2.?
John Smith	1 Cloth Vest	2.00
Adam Corrie	1 Coat	5.62
Same	1 Linen Shirt	1.25
John Milligan	1 Mackinaw Blanket	3.60
Adam Corrie	1 Linen Shirt	1.20
John Milligan	1 Mackinaw Blanket	3.13 or 3.30
Adam Corrie	1 Prime Brothers Vest	_____
Same	1 pair pantaloons	2.?
Mitchell Coll___y	1 Shotgun	8.00
Adam Corrie	1 Vest	1.00
Same	2 Spoons	?

This sale leaves me with more questions than answers. Why didn't the family keep the two blankets? Why did they sell the shotgun? Did they have others, or were they in dire need of funds? And why two spoons?

Brother William was laid to rest in the farm field beside his wife. A simple stone was erected over the graves, but eventually it became covered with brambles and soils. As recently as 1990, descendants of Brother William were still searching for the memorial stone. I was one of those who tried, along with Dallas and his witching wands, to find the graves before the small cemetery at the edge of the field vanished completely from view.

Homemade Pioneer Soap

To make their soap, the pioneers collected grease and lard from their cooking. When they had about 5 pounds they would combine it with lye they obtained by saving ashes in a barrel or hollow log. They would pour water over the ashes and collect it as it drained through, making pure lye. About 2 cups of this lye was put in a big brass or copper kettle, then the 5 pounds of lard and grease, and maybe a little water would be added. A fire was built outdoors, usually surrounded by a circle of rocks upon which they set the kettle. The mixture was boiled for many hours and had to be stirred constantly to keep it from bubbling over. If the mixture started to boil up, a cup of cold water was added to slow the pot. When it began to thicken to the right consistency, the mixture was tested with a spoonful or two placed in a saucer and cooled. If it was the right thickness, it was ready to pour out into pans where it cooled and hardened. The soap was cut into bars and stored to use as needed.

Genealogy Tip 14:
Getting Acquainted with Ancestors

Some genealogists only search out dates, records of marriages, births and deaths and the places where these events happened in the lives of their ancestors. Others—of whom I am one—want to find out as much about their relatives' lives as possible.

One way to get acquainted with people in your past is to read obituaries. The old ones, especially, often go into great detail about an individual's life, experiences, even their likes and dislikes. Wills are another source of background information as you discover land owned, relatives remembered and sometimes grudges and rivalries.

Many counties have published books that include family stories and pictures. It is interesting to read about the lives of your relative's neighbors, details of the communities in which they lived, schools and churches they attended all give you a clearer picture of their lives.

No matter how much background you uncover, a few mysteries always remain. This was true with the progeny of William and Margaret. I learned some from the letters, and a number of the stories handed down through the generations, about interesting experiences of some of my relatives. A researcher has to decide how much of human interest narratives to include in the pages along with the genealogy records. I feel they make far more compelling reading than simple dates and names and places, but each genealogist has to make that decision for himself or herself.

What happened to Brother William and his wife Margaret's children? Little by little I discovered the following:

(1) Son John, William and Margaret's eldest child, stayed in Scotland when the rest of the family emigrated to America. He married a school teacher in Borgue and had a "lawful" son, William, who later came to America and eventually to Iowa. John left his wife, went to London and

lived with a woman there and had more children. In a letter written to his uncle Robert on November 18, 1852, JNO says, *Whilst writing this I received tidings of the death of William's son John. He was the oldest of that family and has left a widow not his lawful wife, I believe, and eight children. He died of a fever. She (his common-law wife) wishes you to let his brothers and sisters know of this.*

William Corrie, son of William's eldest son, John, came to America in the 1850s, and eventually settled in Iowa. Kent Tool photo.

(2) Second son William, Jr., was born circa 1799 in Scotland and was about 23 when he arrived in Illinois. He eventually went to New Orleans, possibly with a shipment of grain. He stayed in Louisiana and became a school teacher. Around 1850 he returned to Illinois about the time the land Adam had purchased was divided up among the relatives. He brought a lady with him who reportedly had dark skin. This sent reverberations through the family as far off as Scotland. Recent information has surfaced that William, Jr., married a woman of the Choctaw Nation. Perhaps this was the woman he brought back with him. After he received his portion of the land, he and his companion returned to New Orleans.

(3) Daughter Margaret was 22 when she married John Milligan in Borgue, Kircudbrightshire, Scotland, just before the beginning of their journey to America. They had their first son 18 months after their arrival in America, followed by five more boys. The 1850 census stated that she lived in Lukin Township with her blind husband John. Her mentally retarded brother George lived with them. Margaret died in 1855 and John in 1868. Both are buried in Bethel cemetery not far from where they built their first home.

(4) Son James was 20 when he made the trip to America. He married a woman named Mary Ann with whom he had seven children. All of the family, except for James and son Henry, died of food poisoning. At the time, however, the story was that a jealous neighbor (identified by some as a witch) had poisoned them. Even the relatives in Britain heard that they had been murdered. My father Carl Corrie told me that story, but two of my Illinois relatives, cousins David Kissel and George Corrie, told me that the deaths were accidental. This is an example of legends that can be perpetrated through the generations. Some of the unfinished or incomplete narratives, however, add interest to the ancestral stories. If we report them in our historical materials, we need to identify them as hearsay.

(5) Adam, 19 when he arrived in the new land, was married the 26th of December in 1823 to his cousin Mary Corrie, daughter of William's brother John and Mary Agnes Corrie. They lived near Bethel church in lower Lawrence County, Lukin Township. Adam became a long-time elder in the Methodist church. Adam and Mary had five children. (Cousins David Kissel, Dallas Krumm, and George Corrie are descendants of Adam and Mary and are proud to be "double Corries.")

(6) Andrew, 16 when the family floated down the Ohio River, was married January 31, 1833 to Elizabeth (Betsy) Schrader. They had 8 children. Andrew died of a "stroke of palsy" in 1872 at age 66. Betsy died of pneumonia in 1889 at 80 years of age. Both are buried in the Bethel Cemetery.

(7) Joseph came across the ocean with his parents when he was 10. He was married in 1835 to Elizabeth Anderson. He died in 1876 and was buried in Bethel cemetery, leaving five children.

(8) Thomas was 8 years old when he came to America. Family records state that he attended classes in the log schoolhouse in his neighborhood. (Perhaps his teacher was Agnes Corrie, Brother John's school teacher daughter.) Thomas worked as a farm hand and then bought a farm of his own in Lukin township where he built a house to which he brought

his bride, Olive Free Moore, in 1834. They had four sons. After Olive's death on 22 June, 1878, Thomas married Olive's widowed sister, Elizabeth A. Moore Lick, in 1880. She died in 1895 and is buried in Bell Cemetery. Thomas died on his 89th birthday in 1904 as he sat under a tree near his home waiting for guests to arrive. He is buried in Bell Cemetery. Thomas and Olive's four sons were James Albert, George Robert, William M., and Thomas Newton (who became my grandfather).

Thomas Corrie, on the right, with his grandson Roy Corrie, son of Thomas Newton Corrie. Thomas Corrie, born in Scotland in 1814, came over with his father, William in 1822.

(9) Jannet (Jane) came to US with her parents at age 7. In 1840, she married Joseph Selby and they had 4 children. She died in 1895.

(10) Mary was 5 years old during the trip to America . She was married in 1835 to William (Bish) Schrader, a teacher of vocal music. Mary died 30 April, 1875, age 57 years; Bish died in 1879; both are buried in Bethel Cemetery. They had one son, Thomas Newton Schrader, who continued to live in the old Schrader home place west of Bethel church. (I have yet to discover where that middle name of Newton came from. A number of Corrie men have it, including my grandfather, Thomas Newton Corrie.)

(11) George was two when the family left Scotland. He was described variously as an invalid, retarded, feebleminded, and even as an idiot. Historian James Corrie explained that George could have been a contributing part of the family. In farming communities many such persons led useful lives, especially in the tending of animals since they didn't need to speak much or at all, and would not have needed to read or write or tell time. They were repaid with loving care and attention. According to the census record, after his mother died

George lived with his sister Margaret. We know he was with her during both the 1850 and 1860 censuses. Despite JNO's letter saying that George should not receive any of Adam's land when it was divided, George must have gotten a share, for his sister reported that George received more attention from other members of the family after he received a portion of the land.

15. Brother Robert

Who is there that does not recollect their first night when started on a long journey. The well-known voices of our friends still ringing in our ears, the parting kiss feels warm still on our lips, and that last separating word, 'FAREWELL' sinks deep into the heart.

—*Lodissa Frizzel*

Many possessions last so much longer than the people who owned them. Descendants of Robert Corrie have a number of items that were his including a small, brassbound wooden writing chest he brought from Scotland, a black paper silhouette of Robert, children's books, and the letters that Robert and his family had received.

Miriam Corrie told me the story of finding those letters at Robert Corrie's home in Wabash County, Illinois, years after Robert's death. Miriam's husband Lester Corrie, a great-grandson of Robert, had gone to see about business near the old homestead. When he returned he handed Miriam a packet of

The cherry wood box and contents brought from Scotland by Brother Robert Corrie in 1828, now owned by descendant Harlan Corrie.

yellowed papers dating back to 1814. "I found these in an old desk. Would you like to have them?" he asked his wife.

Miriam deciphered the quaint handwriting and typed a copy of each page. She added her own handwritten notes summarizing what she had learned and what she suspected about the people who had come to America from Scotland and England, and about those who had stayed behind.

Miriam encouraged Wallace Beals and other relatives to read the letters, and sent me a number of them. She loaned them all to the Illinois State Historical Society to copy for their files. Finally, she gave her son Harlan the originals, along with her transcriptions, and he shared them with me. The letters that Father John, Brother Adam, Nephew JNO, and other relatives wrote to Brother Robert and his wife Sarah give me an insight into life in England and Scotland, and glimpses of what life was like for the immigrant brothers in their Illinois homes.

Miriam Corrie, who saved the old Corrie letters, is seated in front of her family. Her daughter-in-law Judy is on the left. Her granddaughter Lynn is on the right. Standing are, left to right, grandson Chris, son Harlan and Miriam's husband, Lester Corrie, Brother Robert Corrie's great grandson. Photo from Miriam Corrie.

As I read the yellowed pages, I learned more about Brother Robert Corrie, who was born in 1779 in Scotland a year after his Uncle William purchased the land that included South Park. When Robert and his siblings moved with their parents onto that estate, they would have seen the sparkling waters of Brighouse Bay bordering the gently rolling hills covered with green pastures and field flowers. He and his brothers and sister attended the village school in Borgue, and probably went on to study in one of the country's universities.

As a young man Robert traveled to places near London where his brother Adam and his Uncle William were involved in the lace trade. For a time he lived in Olney. Near Olney, at a place called Woburn Sands, he fell in love with Sarah Harbert, a young Quaker woman. They married in 1814.

The earliest of the saved letters was written December 29, 1814, by Father John to Robert and Sarah, who were then in Dublin. It is a long letter that includes much Scripture. Father John's quotations reminded me that this was a time in history when illness and accidents were often life-threatening and religion was sometimes all that people had to help them. *He will never leave thee nor forsake thee*, wrote Father John. *Whom the Lord loveth he chaseteneth, and scourgeth every son and daughter he receiveth . . . We are all on a wilderness journey, may we all be directed by infinite wisdom which cannot err, in the good 'ould way . . . We are at a distance here but our God is everywhere present, and we are secured he will keep that which we commit to him until that day.*

The letter also includes glimpses of the economic situation in Britain. *Markets are very low . . . farmers cannot possibly stand long unless a change comes soon . . .*

Another letter, written about the same time, came from Sarah's brother James Harbert. He refers to financial problems Robert and Sarah were experiencing and tells of his own *The lace business you know was so bad I wanted to make a trial of something else . . . The meal business and farming I have found (to be) much worse. Times and circumstances which were impossible to foresee operate against them both. The villages are terribly poor . . . time is gone for prosperity in old England.*

A letter to Mrs. Robert Corrie dated August 19, 1815, was sent to High Street, Wellingborough, suggesting that Robert and Sarah were back in England and that Robert had resumed his work as a lace dealer in Wellingborough and Olney. It also indicates that Robert and Sarah were moving from place to place. Were they restless? Was business so bad that they kept looking for a more promising location?

The first mention of the possibility of a Corrie emigrating to America is in the same letter: *Adam Corrie, it is said, continues in the same mind respecting America . . .*

Robert and Sarah had their first child, Sarah, who died. Then they had a son, James, and then another son, John Robert.

In 1818, Adam's wife Penelope wrote to Sarah telling of her own baby's death. Penelope commented that she hoped that Sarah and Robert's sons would be spared a similar fate. Her writing vividly shows the fear of every parent in that period in history, for many children died at birth or soon after. Penelope also mentions that Robert *had an argument with Brother Adam and gave up his part of the business,* evidence that Robert and Adam worked together at least for a time as business partners, but had parted ways.

By then Brother Adam's son JNO had been to America and purchased the land in Illinois for his father. Adam then encouraged his brothers to emigrate. Robert's brother John left Scotland in 1919, and his Brother William emigrated in 1822, but Robert and Sarah would wait six more years before deciding to make the journey.

Sarah gave birth to another child, Margaret, who soon died. Sarah's sister Elizabeth mentions the death of the baby in an 1826 letter to Sarah. *I was not prepared for such news as your letter contained . . . I had hoped that dear little Margaret was better. Indeed I thought she might out-grow her complaint. It did not strike me that I should see her no more . . . Sweet child, thou and the sister spirit are now completely happy. I do indeed feel keenly on your account but though Sarah be not, and Margaret be not . . . they are (experiencing no pain). The briars of the wilderness, the thorns of the desert which wound so deeply as to make us remember we are still in the wilderness. Your pleasant gourds are withered. You have lost a promising part of your little family . . . and now you are retracing these scenes of joy during their short sojourn on earth.*

Another letter from Sarah's family that same year mentions *your approaching trial,* a suggestion that Sarah was pregnant again. Sarah eventually had a daughter Jane, born June 4, 1827.

Sometime during all these family experiences, the idea to follow his two brothers to America became a reality for Robert and Sarah. They packed their belongings, including the fine brassbound wooden box, added the medicines JNO suggested, and put in a few lemons and oranges as antidotes to seasickness. When all was in readiness, Father John held a farewell party for them in his South Park home.

Robert was so deeply saddened at the idea of leaving his family and childhood home that he could not stand to say good-bye. While others were enjoying the festivities, he slipped away from the warmth of the fire in the parlor hearth, the sweets on the table in the dining room, and the black marble bowl filled with bright colored fruits. He walked away unseen, knowing he would never again be with any of these people he loved so much.

As Robert stumbled down the hill, did he turn and look back at the manor house surrounded with trees? Was he already aching with love for his parents and the country where he had grown to manhood? Did the setting sun shining on the window panes cast a golden reflection that intensified the pain in his heart?

Robert's failure to say good-bye hurt all his relatives. Brother Adam wrote to Robert in May of 1828: *I cannot forgive myself for being put off my guard, in believing fully that you would in a manly and brotherly and friendly way shake hands with each of us and say farewell. I had just gone out and decanted a very fine bottle of old Madeira with which I meant to treat you and the family previous to leaving, when lo and behold my wife came in and announced with a sorrowful countenance your departure . . . There was scarcely a dry eye in the house and the depression is still visible . . . I earnestly and affectionately commend you and your wife and your children into the hands of that being who slumbers not nor sleeps . . . and will bring you all to safety by a right way to a city of habitation.*

Brother Adam concluded his letter, *I am more and more satisfied that the purchasing of the American Estate was under Providence to become a blessing as well as a nursery to those of our (family) and friends who could not obtain in this country a remuneration for all their toils. I trust you and yours may have many happy years in prospect and know that no friend you have on earth will more rejoice in it than myself . . . Whatever is in my power to add to your happiness shall be done.*

For several years Adam and JNO wrote scolding messages to Robert for not giving them the pleasure of saying good-bye. Despite the pain he had caused, Robert's actions never pushed a wedge between him and his father. Father John sent books for his grandchildren, and included notes to all of them . . . *my best wishes for your happiness and that of all who accompany you on your long journey . . . May he who only can protect you hide you under the shadow of his wings and guide you in safety to your destination and provide you with every comfort on your arrival in a foreign land . . .*

Robert, Sarah and their children followed the pattern of Robert's two older brothers by sailing from Liverpool, England. After several weeks on the high seas, they landed in Baltimore, Maryland, and bought or rented wagons and horses or oxen to carry their family and possessions overland to Pittsburgh where they arranged passage down the Ohio River.

While the family was in Pittsburgh they suffered the loss of their eldest son James from a fever. It is ironic that he died in the same city and in the same manner as his cousin Penelope, Brother John's daughter, ten years earlier. Robert would have been busy getting their houseboat purchased or built and the supplies for their trip obtained, and I hope pushed his sorrow down under all the activity. But what of Sarah? How did she cope as she cared first for her dying son, and then comforted her remaining small children, John Robert and Jane? It must have been searingly painful, alone in a strange land, without the loving presence of relatives or long-time friends to give her comfort.

The next letter in Miriam's collection is dated October 24, 1829, and was sent to Robert Corrie in care of the Corrieville post office, Mt. Carmel, Edwards County, Illinois. From it we know that Robert and his family had arrived on Corrie lands and the hard work of getting settled would have begun. They had to erect a house and farm buildings, buy supplies, and make what they could by their own efforts. The families of John and William would have helped Robert and Sarah get established in the community. The fact that this youngest brother was the last to come surely made his family's integration into the new way of life easier than it had been for his older brothers.

The knowledge that Robert and his Sarah had to do their own mundane tasks bothered their Scottish and English relatives. A letter from Elizabeth Davidson, Sarah's sister, written October 24, 1829 says *Dear Sister: Is not this your birthday? . . . You've been in peril on land and peril at*

*sea . . . (and now) I am sorry you cannot get more assistance for your house . . .
and I sincerely sympathize with you in all your privations. Love to baby Jane.*

Another letter from Sarah's sister, written in 1834, continues the
refrain. (Note the Quaker use of *thee* and *thou* and *thy*.) *I cannot think
how thou can perform all thy domestic engagements . . . This lies with great
weight on my mind and I think thy life is one of toil and drudgery . . . I should
be glad on thine own account and also thy husbands if thee could be relieved
of the hard labour . . . I very much feel the indisposition of thy husband and
hope his recovery and his health is established long before this reaches you.*
(The letter does not elaborate on why Robert's health is mentioned.)

Several other letters tell that Adam's wife Penelope was handing
down clothes to Sarah and Robert. She also sent new material and
money for hats, and clothing for a funeral.

After settling in America, the family prepared for at least two more
babies. Neither of these babies lived to be recorded. Did people of
that time in history feel that ignoring such a birth would make it less
painful than acknowledging a child's existence? Regardless of the pre-
vailing custom, mothers have a way of forever holding a deep sadness
in their hearts over such a loss.

The British relatives wrote at length about their hope that the families in Illinois had medical help near at hand, not realizing the scarcity
of care on the frontier.

In one of her letters Penelope wrote to her sister-in-law Sarah her
repeated refrain, *Never, I beseech you as you advance in life, give up your
authority as a wife, parent or mistress of your own family. For peace I have
given up . . .* The letter becomes illegible from there on. I'll never know
what drove Penelope to make that statement.

The family in Scotland also worried about the status of their American relatives. This concern was evident when Mr. Foster, a friend of

Sarah's, came over from Scotland to Illinois with thoughts of settling there. When he got to the Corrie neighborhood, he saw a man feeding his hogs. "Where is your master?" he asked,

"I am the master," the man replied. It was Robert Corrie himself.

Mr. Foster wrote back to an acquaintance in England: *I have no intention of settling in Illinois. Why, Squire Corrie himself was slopping his hogs!*

Robert and Sarah were managing fairly well with their Illinois venture. Several letters from British relatives made the comment that *we are happy for your success in America.* Indeed Robert doubled his holdings when he purchased an additional 100 acres, and later another 90 acres.

However, Robert was not exempt from being scolded by his Brother Adam and nephew JNO. Adam wrote several letters in the 1830s saying, *If I cannot have the tax paid on time and the timber cared for I have a mind to send out an agent at once to sell the whole of my property in your quarter for the best price that can be procured and forever after wash my hands of America . . .*

Robert Corrie's barnyard in Wabash County, Illinois, circa 1860s. Harlan Corrie photo.

In 1838 JNO wrote to Robert, *It does seem very desirable that every one who has a part of the land which was my father's should have it entered in his own name at the tax office. My father ought no longer to be responsible for the payment of tax on land which does not belong to him—besides which it encumbers and perplexes the accounts.* By that time JNO and Brother Adam obviously considered the Illinois land to be the property of the settlers.

Robert and Sarah also continued their religious leanings. They entertained ministers who came their way, had preaching done in their home, and followed the admonition of their relatives who wrote in their letters, *I hope you have some enjoyment the first day of the week in the small circle in which you move.* The British relatives searched for ministers and teachers to send to the little community in Illinois.

Robert and Sarah's daughter Jane was married in 1856 to Samuel Baldridge, a Presbyterian minister, who served the Wabash Presbyterian church. Jane helped her husband found a college. She taught classes, boarded and roomed students in their home, and washed and ironed her husband's white shirts (he seldom wore anything else). An accomplished seamstress, she was often asked to sew burial garments for deceased babies and children. She bore five children and suffered the loss of three for whom she grieved all her life. She also raised two orphaned grandchildren.

On my first trip to Illinois I stood in the Wabash graveyard near the Presbyterian church at the place once known as Corrieville, whose first congregation Brother Adam helped fund.

George Corrie and Evelyn besides Robert and Sarah Corrie's tombstone in the Wabash graveyard.

I found the tall stone with the names of Jane Corrie and Samuel Baldridge and the sad litany of their children who had preceded them in death. Nearby I found the memorial to Brother John and his wife Mary Agnes, the marker moved from the farm field where they lie buried near the site of their pioneer log cabin. Between the two grave stones was a third, that of Robert and Sarah.

The stones were monuments dedicated to people who have become real to me as I'd gathered the stories of their struggles and sorrows, their delights and successes. But I walked away from the cemetery with an aching heart, for there was no marker in that place to indicate that the other Corrie brother, my great-great-grandfather William, had ever existed.

Cock-a-leekie Soup

This recipe is well-known in Britain. Versions of it came to America with the Corrie families to be used with wild birds or with farm-raised chickens.

1 chicken

3 pounds potatoes, peeled and diced

1 pound leeks or onions, peeled and diced

1/2 pound celery, diced

1/2 cup butter (or margarine)

8 cups chicken stock

Salt and pepper to taste

Put the chicken in a kettle. Cover with water and put on lid. Cook until meat is tender. Remove chicken and let cool. Remove meat from bone and cut into bite-sized pieces. Combine potatoes, leeks (or onions) and celery in a large kettle; add chicken stock and butter and simmer until vegetables are tender. Season as desired and add chicken pieces. Heat and serve hot. Makes 12 servings.

Genealogy Tip 15: Meaningful Contacts

When I was in the Heinz Pittsburgh Regional History Center in Pittsburgh, I tried to find information about Pittsburgh's earliest cemeteries, hoping to discover the place where two of the Corrie brothers' children lie buried. My search was fruitless: the cemeteries I did contact had no reference to burials or names as far back as 1819 and 1828. Research can be frustrating!

The Regional History Center provided me with background material that gave me a sense of the lives of the three brothers who emigrated from Scotland. As I read stories of other pioneer's experiences they helped me visualize my Corrie relatives struggles and challenges. It was a meaningful contact.

Keepsakes can be meaningful contacts as well. Letters are especially precious. Sarah, the gentle Quaker lady whose relatives always worried that her work in her pioneer home was difficult, treasured every missive arriving from the loved ones overseas. She saved each pressed flower, every piece of ribbon, and all the books that came to the family. Caring for artifacts today is a loving service as thoughtful relatives strive to preserve their heritage for those who follow.

I found no letters written from the British relatives to Brothers John or William. Surely they wrote to them as well, but their families obviously didn't save them as Robert's family had. We do not have copies of any letters the three sons of Father John and his wife Margaret wrote to their relatives in Britain, a real loss in learning more about their experiences in this new land. However, I rejoice in what I have read and in the willingness of Miriam Corrie and her son Harlan to share with me and with others.

Stories found in letters, diaries, and journals are important for historians who want to find details of the lives of people during certain historical periods and places. Allowing relatives and historians to use the Corrie letters was a gift that I consider priceless.

As my own research went deeper into Robert and Sarah's family I was frustrated with how little I knew about most of their children. What could just a birthday and death date tell me?

This lack of detail made me read between the lines as I tried to visualize the experiences of the family with early deaths, the grief they suffered as they lost several children, of the struggles to find adequate medical care in the wilderness areas. Starting with the facts, I made an emotional contact with these relatives.

No one ever explained to me that a genealogical tool can sometimes be a person's imagination. I realized that a major contact was my own mind, as I discovered how to use it in a meaningful way.

Actual information about Robert and Sarah's family include the following:

Robert died in 1863 and Sarah died in 1865; they are buried in the Wabash Cemetery in Orio, Illinois (once known as Corrieville.)

Robert and Sarah had the following children:

(1) Sarah, died in England in 1826 or before.

(2) Margaret died as an infant.

Possibly another baby who died at birth.

(3) James, born in England (no date recorded), and died 1828 in Pittsburgh, Pennsylvania, on the way to Illinois.

(4) John Robert, born 1816. Came to America with his parents at age 12. Married first to Elizabeth Beesley who was born in 1822. She died in childbirth in 1852 leaving one son, James Robert. John Robert secondly married Elizabeth Cynthia Thompson. They had eight children.

(5) Another child named Margaret died before her parents came to America and was buried 23 January, 1826, in the Baptist Church in Cranfield, Bedfordshire, England.

(6) Jane, born 4 June 1826, baptized in the Baptist Church in Cranfield, Bedfordshire, England. Emigrated to America with her family when she was 2. Married 1856 to Rev. Samuel Baldridge. They had 5 children. The eldest was (1) Herbert, who died before his parents. Jane and Samuel helped raise Herbert's children—Bessie, Mayo, and Earl, (2) Sarah died age 15, (3) Samuel died age 12, (4) Mary lived to adulthood and had two sons, (5) Harriett died at 10 months.

The Rev. Samuel Baldridge died in Hanover Indiana, 15 April 1898. Jane died 28 February 1903. They and four of their children are buried near Jane's father and mother in the Wabash Cemetery.

16. The Family Reunion

Hope focused settlers' attention on tomorrow, helped them to endure present tribulations, and gave them meaning to suffering. Very likely, hope was the settlers' greatest resource.

—James Edward Davis

By the mid-1990s, I had discovered so many pieces of my family puzzle one would think I would be satisfied to stop my search, but I still wanted to find exactly where William was buried and pay him homage.

I finished putting together a genealogy book of all I had discovered about the Corries. It contained material from historians Jessie Corrie and James Corrie, the bits and pieces from my father, notes from Wallace Beals, and information from the letters saved by Miriam Corrie. I included pictures and notes from my cousins Olivia, Gladys and Dallas.

Following my first trip to eastern Illinois and the Corrie lands in 1993, the idea began taking shape in my mind for a family reunion. With the help of Corrie descendants David Kissel, George Corrie, Dallas Krumm, and Anna Rae Anderson, who live near where Corrieville (later *Orio*) had been located, we began planning the event.

It took several years to prepare. Then, on Labor Day weekend of 1995, Corrie kin from Oregon, Arizona, Texas, Seattle, and the Illinois towns of Freeport, Peoria, Lawrenceville, Mt. Carmel, and Rushville gathered at the place settled by the three Corrie brothers in the early 1800s. The date for the reunion coincided with Chowder Day, held every Labor Day weekend in the place now known as the community of Orio, Illinois, in a grove of trees across the road from the Wabash Presbyterian Church.

Community and family celebrations in Illinois have long been built around steaming kettles of soup known by the names *burgoo*, *stew*, *barbecue*, and *chowder*. It contains ingredients the local people found appropriate, tasty, and available. In the early days, those could include squirrel, quail, wild turkey, and raccoon brought in by hunters. The cooks added vegetables from their gardens or their supplies of canned goods, and simmered the soup in big iron kettles nestled in a trench filled with hot coals. The chowder could take hours or even days to cook.

The tradition continues today. Hundreds of people from near and far attend the Orio Chowder. They wander the grounds, shop for handmade craft items, and enjoy the games, stunts, speeches, and music. Mostly, though, they come to visit and eat chowder.

On the day of our reunion, the Chowder Day committee had erected a large tent to shelter tables that held dishpans filled with ingredients ready to go into the cooking pots. I peeked underneath the newspapers laid over the tops of the pans and saw carrots, celery, onions and beans.

And talk about kettles! Eleven large metal vats stood on the cement floor under a nearby wooden-roofed shelter. Each vat was filled with seventy-five gallons of vegetables and meat. The electrical stirring mechanisms, looking like giant beaters, were fastened to a rail over-head, and a gas jet underneath each kettle provided the heat. We watched as a crew stirred the mix with long wooden paddles to help keep the ingredients evenly distributed. The soup had been cooking since before dawn.

By midmorning people were lining up near the tent where helpers were selling chowder in bulk. Each purchaser carried a container of some sort—a pressure cooker, canning kettle, pan, or bucket—ready to have it filled with chowder for ten dollars a gallon. Most planned to take their chowder home and freeze it for future meals.

One of the Orio Chowder's large metal cooking vats with its long stirring mechanism is admired by Robert, Craig, Evelyn and Sharon Birkby.

At another tent, volunteers sold bowls of soup to be eaten on the grounds, along with a variety of drinks, cakes, pies, ice cream, plus hamburgers and fish sandwiches. People took their food to tables under the trees where they could dine and take part in the entertainment.

Tent and tables under the trees where the Orio chowder is served to the public.

My husband Robert, our sons Jeff and Craig, and our daughter-in-law Sharon joined me as we enjoyed our lunch. A performer named Cowboy Lee, dressed in blue jeans and a bright plaid western shirt, tried to keep from falling off the back of the hay-wagon stage as he twirled lassos, cracked whips, told stories, and sang cowboy songs. Later, he preached a fire-and-brimstone sermon to the visitors in the grove. He was definitely a reincarnation of the circuit-riding ministers of old.

By two o'clock our reunion people were well fed and ready for adventure. I had set up a place in a nearby building for the Corries to register. Seventy-five people stopped by to sign in, get the schedule of our activities, collect the T-shirts and sweat shirts embroidered with the Corrie crest and motto, pick up their genealogy books, sign the guest book, and tour the local trails of our forebears.

We visited two churches steeped in Corrie history. The first was Bethel Methodist Church. The construction had been financed by Margaret Corrie Schrader, daughter of Brother John and Mary Agnes, who went on horseback around the countryside to collect money to build it. By the time Margaret started her project, a number of the Scottish Presbyterian Corries had become Methodists due to the successes of that denomination's circuit riders. After we saw the interior of the church, Corrie descendants David Kissel and George Corrie guided us to the cemetery behind the house of worship where they pointed out the gravestones of interest and told us about those

Corrie relatives go into the Bethel church during the reunion road trip.

"Double cousins" George Corrie and David Kissel stand in the Bethel cemetery behind the stone dedicated to their ancestors Adam Corrie (Brother William's son) and his wife Mary Corrie (Brother John's daughter).

buried there including their "double ancestors," Mary and Adam Corrie.

The second church was Olive Branch Methodist, a small frame structure that is very special place for me. Part of my great-grandfather Thomas's family helped build the church and then attended services there. Several of his family members are buried in the tiny adjacent graveyard.

We stopped briefly at all that is left of the house my great-grandfather Thomas Corrie built and where he raised his four sons, including my grandfather. Long empty and falling into disrepair, it still gave us a sense of the simple nature of the early Corrie homes. I looked at the large trees by the lane and wondered which tree Thomas sat beneath on his 89th birthday as he watched for his relatives to appear for his surprise party. When the guests did arrive, they were the ones surprised, for Thomas had quietly slipped away into eternity.

Olive Branch church, a sacred place for the Corrie family.

Next, our tour took us up a rutted lane to the neatly-kept Bell cemetery where Thomas lies buried. We were sorry to see that the top of his memorial stone had broken off and resting at an angle against the base, something that happens to many old markers in pioneer burial grounds.

Cousin Dallas had come prepared. He unloaded repair equipment from his truck and, with many helpful Corrie hands, smoothed the foundation of Thomas' stone, slathered on glue, and put the tall top of the marker back into place.

Relatives reconstruct the broken monument stone of Thomas Corrie in the Bell Cemetery.

Later in the afternoon, we came near the place where brothers John and William had settled their families. At that moment I wondered if William had been happy with his choice to come to this new land and start a different kind of life for himself and his large family.

It was time for Cousin Dallas, with permission of the landowner, to guide us through a field of drying soy beans.

"We are getting near the old Corrie burying grounds," he said, as the line of relatives moved toward a curve in a creek. I could hear the crunch of the crisp leaves underfoot and the sound of birds in the nearby trees and sensed that something important was about to happen.

Dallas showed us how to witch for graves using his clothes hanger bent into two L-shapes. With one of the wands in each hand and held

A line of Corries traipsing across the soybean field toward the primitive burial ground of their ancestors.

out before him, Dallas walked slowly ahead. The tips of the wands pointed forward, holding steady. "I know we are close," he said to the eager faces around him. "We are very close." Just then the wands in his hands crossed each other, a movement Dallas said was caused by fluctuations in the earth's magnetic field caused by the presence of graves. "This has

Dallas Krumm with his witching wand.

to be the place where Margaret and William are buried and near-by are William's brother John and his wife Mary Agnes. Hush. Listen for the voices."

We stood in silence, lost in thought. A breeze rustled the leaves in the trees. I could hear the quiet breathing of those standing near me in that moment of reflection. I was aware of a closeness to William, a sense of his presence. I felt the strength, courage, and determination it had taken for him to leave his homeland for a place so far away and about which he knew so little.

No longer was this simply a soybean field with rows of stalks that ended on a barren patch of ground beside a bramble-covered stream. To me, this small corner of the peaceful field was a hallowed place. With the help of witching wands and the letters and records of relatives through the generations, I had found where William's great American adventure had come to a close.

Orio Chowder

Phoebe Jackman of Allendale, Illinois, a descendant of Brother Robert Corrie, helps each year with Orio Chowder Days. She gave me the following recipes. The first is the large recipe they put together in the big vats for the annual celebration. The second is her smaller, "family-sized" version.

10 pounds beef
2 pounds suet
3 hens or 4 chickens
1 dishpan full cabbage
1 dishpan full diced potatoes
1 dishpan full tomatoes, cut
Corn, not so much

Generous gallon of onions
Beans of all kinds (a dishpan
    full but no more)
Carrots, and a few turnips or
    sweet potatoes
Celery will do no harm
Water, as needed

Put ingredients together. Cook and stir a long time, until flavors blend and everything is tender. Season as desired. Makes a good-sized kettle full.

Smaller Orio Chowder

Just in case you'd like something a little smaller and more accurate in its measurements, cousin Phoebe also gave me this second recipe:

3 whole chickens
3 lbs. beef chunks
1 peck potatoes
2 gallons tomatoes
3 heads cabbage
1 gallon onions

2 gallon beans
1/2 gallon butter beans
4 dozen ears of corn
Salt and pepper to taste
Noodles, rice, or spaghetti
Water, as needed

Cook according to directions in first recipe, adding noodles, rice, or spaghetti about 20 minutes before the end of the cooking time.

Homemade Noodles

5 cups flour
6 eggs

1 Tablespoon half-and-half
1 teaspoon butter

Put flour into a large bowl. Make a depression, a well, in the center and add all the rest of the ingredients in the well. Mix with a fork or your fingers to incorporate as much of the flour into the liquid ingredients as possible. Shape into a ball, knead several times, and roll out on a floured board until thin. Let dry about 20 minutes, then cut into narrow strips. Shake out onto a lightly floured counter or bread board and cover with a clean tea towel. Let dry for several hours. Cook in salted chicken broth, or in the chowder mixture, until noodles are tender—15 to 20 minutes. These noodles freeze well. Put uncooked meal portions in plastic bags or freezer jars and freeze until time to drop into the hot broth and cook. The recipe can also be cut to make a smaller amount, just as the chowder can.

Genealogy Tip 16: Planning Family Reunions

To plan a family reunion, start early. Two years may not be too long. If possible, have a steering committee to head it up, then get as many people involved as you can. Designate tasks. It should be a group effort.

Collect names and addresses. Send out questionnaires that will give relatives opportunities to suggest the time when, and location where, the reunion might be held. It could be a place of family history such as the site of our Corrie gathering, or a central location, or a hotel or cruise line, or other business that caters to family groups. A small reunion could be held in someone's home.

Decide what you want to visit—churches, cemeteries, historical spots near where the reunion is to be held. In your invitations include maps and suggested transportation options and information on places to stay.

Organize the schedule and include printed copies with the invitations. When the invitations finally go out, be certain that everyone in the celebrated family line(s) gets one.

Plan food. The chowder at the Corrie family reunion was perfect for our first meal. The owners of the Poor Farm Bed-and-Breakfast in Mt. Carmel, where a number of Corrie relatives stayed, provided our breakfasts, our Saturday evening picnic, and our Sunday lunch.

Publicize in newspapers, via a newsletter, through e-mail, and by calling people on the telephone to remind them of deadlines for making reservations.

Tell the relatives what you want them to bring such as photographs of family past and present, memorabilia, and any genealogical records they might have.

If possible, plan a project. For the Corries, it involved raising money for a new memorial stone for William and Margaret and dedicating it at the reunion.

Repairing old cemetery stones is an excellent project. The tools and supplies to repair stones are simple: epoxy glue, a spade, a rake, a wire brush to clean broken surfaces, and a caulking gun. Check the internet for more details on gravestone repair.

Another popular project for reunions is a family cookbook. The organizing committee can ask people to send their family favorites early so that they can be included in a book available at the reunion, or ask the participants to bring their recipes to the reunion and print the book later. (Those books can be ordered at the reunion so the committee will know how many to print.)

Some reunions make a family quilt. Families can make their quilt blocks ahead of time, or be provided with squares of fabric and textile paint at the reunion and encouraged to design blocks. This is a great activity for children. Arrange for someone to put the quilt together and decide where it will be kept. Raffling off the quilt can provide money for a worthy project, a charity, or to help fund the next reunion.

Plan the place for registration. We had tables in a building near the chowder tent where the Corries could register, get their name tags, pick up their family genealogy books, and the T-shirts that they had ordered earlier. We had extras available for people who had not pre-ordered.

Set up a table for attendees to display family memorabilia—historic photos, military medals, old jewelry, family Bibles, etc. To safeguard treasured items, be sure everything is labeled and that the table is always hosted.

Include photo opportunities at the reunion. Take pictures of family groups and of the entire gathering, record the name and address of everyone shown in each photo. Video cameras and digital cameras make picture taking simple. Sharing the pictures later is an important way to stay in touch.

Plan plenty of time to visit. A storytelling hour can encourage the sharing of family memories. If everyone agrees, have someone videotape this session.

Arrange activities for the children. Hay rides, scavenger hunts, softball or volleyball, and hikes are just a few of the possibilities. If some relative is artistic, create a coloring picture book telling some of the family's stories. Duplicate this for the children and provide them with crayons. Print extras, since adults will want copies, too.

Determine your budget and method of payment. Calculate all your costs before the reunion and decide if you are going to ask for a contribution from each person who comes and how much is needed. Include this in the invitation. Surplus funds can be used to plan the next reunion or develop a project.

Conduct an evaluation. When almost everyone else had gone after our noon luncheon following the gravestone dedication, Dallas Krumm, David Kissel, and I sat down and talked about the reunion and where we would go from there, especially with our Corrie Family Records. Soon afterward we found Tim Corrie, Jr., a computer specialist who graciously agreed to continue the keeping and publications of our family records.

Afterword

"And yet, in a larger and truer sense, we are all keepers of the story, for the blood that flows in our veins is the blood of immigrant forebears who sacrificed mightily to carve a new life in a brave, new world."

—Steven Berntsen

I t was a beautiful autumn Sunday of the Corrie family reunion when the relatives gathered to dedicate William and Margaret's new memorial stone. The sky was so clear and bright blue it seemed to lift to the far reaches of heaven. Tiny wisps of clouds floated near the horizon. A light breeze was blowing from the south across the nearby grove where the crowds had gathered for chowder the day before.

As I walked from the car toward the church, a squirrel chattered in the tree over my head, wondering, no doubt, at this intruder into its territory. Crickets chirping in the dry grass hopped out of my way. In the distance I heard the bark of a dog and realized a farm was nearby, perhaps in Decker's Prairie, the place near Corrieville where William had built his American home.

Two years before our reunion, Corrie descendants had begun contributing funds to purchase and erect a memorial to William and Margaret. With the help of cousin Anna Rae Anderson who lived nearby, we purchased a new stone and arranged to have it placed in the cemetery row near John and Robert's gravestones. Even if the location of their actual graves was lost forever, the two would still be remembered.

Many of the Corrie reunion visitors attended services that Sunday morning in the stone church next to the cemetery. The speaker was Cowboy Lee, the evangelist who had twirled ropes and cracked whips the day before. I imagined myself back in the pioneer days of revival meetings.

After the church service, the relatives gathered near the gravestones of the Corrie brothers. My sons Craig and Jeff Birkby arranged one set of the helium-filled balloons at each of the three brothers' stones. The balloons were purple to remind us of the colorful heather and thistles of Scotland. My daughter-in-law Sharon handed out the programs for the service and my husband Robert helped some of the older folks walk across the uneven ground. A bagpipe player in full Scottish regalia stood beside the new memorial stone. He lifted the mouthpiece, blew in air until the bag under his left arm inflated, and as the first plaintive notes sounded, the dedication began.

Corrie kin gathering in the Wabash Presbyterian church cemetery for the dedication of William and Margaret's stone.

Standing beside the piper as he finished his introductory number, I turned to welcome those present. *We are here in the land to which our forebears came 173 years ago. Much has happened since they arrived. Much has changed, including the fact that there are far more Corrie folks populating this country than when the three brothers, John, William and Robert, and their families built their first log cabins. One hundred and seventy three years is a long, long time, and yet I have the feeling that today we are reaching back through the decades to touch the lives of those of our family who first came to America.*

The Scottish piper, Robert Cunningham and Evelyn Corrie Birkby wait for the ceremony to begin.

That sense of family remains strong. We are truly surrounded by a great crowd of witnesses. In my mind, heaven is not far away and those we see around us here are only a small number of the Corries and their kin who are touching us at this moment with their love.

Father John must have felt strong emotions when he saw three of his sons and their families leave Scotland knowing they would never meet again. They came with faith that a better life awaited them here, and we hope that they enjoyed enough good experiences to balance out the hard work, the sorrows, and the disappointments.

Last year my sons Bob and Jeff and I traveled to Scotland where we tried to get a sense of the earliest Corries. As we stood on the steps at South Park, the ancestral manor house, I imagined what Father John must have felt as he stood on those same steps and looked toward America and wondered how his sons were faring.

In one letter sent from America to Brother Adam, Brother Robert enclosed a spray of grass from the graves of brothers John and William. This gave me the idea to pick some heather and flowers from the South Park pastures and bring them back here to make into sprays to place today on the stones for John, for Robert, and on the newly erected memorial for William and Margaret.

Gladys Corrie Illingworth placing a spray of flowers beside William and Margaret's new gravestone. Brother John's marker is on the right.

Descendant of each of the brothers placed a spray of field flowers and heather on the respective stones—Virginia Corrie-Cozart on John's, Harlan Corrie on Robert's, and Gladys Corrie Illingworth on William's.

Anna Rae Anderson, who had helped so much with the planning of the reunion, gave the closing prayer: We give thanks, our father, that you guided our ancestors safely over land and ocean, that in your kindly providence you brought them to this pleasant place, and that we, as a result of their courage, are privileged to live in this land founded under God.

We give thanks that this country was settled by men and women like those we honor today who came so they could live and worship in freedom according to the dictates of their consciences.

Help us never to forget that all we enjoy today was earned through sacrifice and struggle of these Corrie brothers and their families. Their strong heritage is ours and we ask that we may never regard it lightly.

We are thankful for Your constant presence in our lives and pray in humbleness and thanksgiving as we dedicate this stone to the loving memory of our ancestors, William and Margaret Corrie. Amen

Brother William and his wife Margaret's new memorial marker in Wabash Presbyterian cemetery, Orio, IL. Dedicated during the Corrie reunion.

The piper played "Amazing Grace," and Jeff and Craig released the balloons from each gravestone, one at a time. As the purple orbs rose over the broad fields that stretch north of the cemetery, land where the first Corrie families had built their log cabins so long ago, we stood in a circle and held hands. I was touched by a sense of the closeness of those present, and those only in spirit, and tears began to course down my cheeks. I looked at those around me and realized that almost everyone in that circle was crying as well.

The last skirl of the bagpipe faded away as we said our final good-byes. My family began to load up our car with items left from the event as I stood alone beside William's stone. I let my mind return to other cemeteries I had visited—the graveyard in Terregles next to the two-part church where I found the graves of William of Clunie, of his sons Alexander and John, and of his grandson "Obstinate" Adam. I remembered the depth of emotion in Borgue when I found Father John's marker, and the flush of delight when Jeff discovered the one of Father John's brother, Uncle William (both sons of Obstinate Adam).

I looked down the simple line of gravestones in front of me, the memorials for three of Father John's sons, Uncle William's nephews, and Brother Adams siblings. Here were Brother John and Mary Agnes' stone moved from the farm field, the tall marker of Brother Robert and Sarah, and the new rectangular one for Brother William and Margaret. I thought of that abandoned burial grounds in the farm field with its pioneer graves that we had finally found with simple witching wands. I knew that my William would never be lost again.

It suddenly occurred to me what I should do with all my experiences and memories. I imagined that I once again held the old black marble bowl from South Park in my hands. Inside its smooth interior I placed every experience, every special moment, and the people I had met during my search, including those we had just honored in the cemetery in the place once known as Corrieville. I gently blanketed them all with my love and carried them with me as I walked to the car and my waiting family.

People Important to this Story

▨ **William Corrie** of Clunie. *(No birth date.) Died between 1700 and 1717.*

└─▨ **John Corrie,** William's eldest son. *Born 1663, died 1712.*

└─▨ **"Obstinate" Adam,** John Corrie's son. *Born 1703, died 1786*

Two of Obstinate Adam's sons:

└─▨ **Uncle William,** *born 1735, died 1811,* and

▨ **Father John,** *born 1739, died 1829.*

Father John's children:

└─▨ **Brother Adam,** *who earned the money and sent his son JNO to America to buy land in Illinois. Adam was born in 1770 and died in 1846.*

▨ **Brother John,** *the first of the Corrie brothers to come to America in 1819. Born 1773 died 1823.*

▨ **Brother William,** *the author's lost ancestor, the second brother to arrive in Illinois came in 1822. Born 1766 died 1835.*

▨ **Brother Robert,** *the last of the three brothers to emigrate, came in 1828. Born 1779, died 1863.*

└─▨ **Thomas Corrie,** *who came to America from Scotland in 1822 with his father, William. Born 1814 died 1904.*

└─▨ **Thomas Newton Corrie,** *the youngest of Thomas' four sons. Born 1846, died 1922.*

└─▨ **Carl M. Corrie,** *Son of Thomas Newton Corrie. Born 1881 died 1942.*

└─▨ **Evelyn Corrie Birkby,** *daughter of Carl. Born in 1919. Went looking for her lost ancestor William.*

Corrie family crest
and motto
"Vigilant and Audacious"

Acknowledgments

My thanks to all those who have done research and recording of the Corrie family history including historian James Corrie of England; my Scottish cousins Sandra and John Corrie; my father Carl Corrie; my grandmother Nancy Edmondson Corrie; my grandfather Thomas Newton Corrie; Wallace Beals and his son; and my cousins Olivia Doner and Gladys Corrie Illingworth, who shared their photographs and stories.

To Miriam Corrie who kept telling me, "Someone should write this story," as she shared some of the old letters with me, and her son Harlan Corrie who allowed me to read his copies of Jessie Corrie's books and the full collection of the early letters, and who shared pictures from his own trips to Scotland. His original watercolor painting of South Park is a treasure.

To the people along the way including Margaret and Tom Brown, Mrs. Parker, and the man by the side of the road. To Thomas Corrie Gillespie and his father Douglas Gillespie. To Anna Rae Anderson, George Corrie, David Kissel, Dallas Krumm and John King who helped with my research and the family reunion in Illinois.

To the helpful staffs of historical libraries and genealogy centers including the Edinburgh Historical Library, Latter Day Saints Family Centers, Pittsburgh Historical Library, the Mississippi Queen, and various county historical and genealogy centers. To Iowa poet Michael Carey for his enthusiastic guidance during the latter stages of my work. To Amy Smith for her graphic design work on the cover and interior pages.

Finally, my love and deep appreciation to my three sons Bob, Jeff, and Craig, who went with me on some of my adventures to find William and who helped with their encouragement and suggestions through the years I have been writing this book. Additional thanks to Bob and Jeff, who did much of the editing of the manuscript and then shepherded it to publication and helped me make a real book into a great one.

Bibliography

Doniger, Wendy. *Splitting the Difference*. Chicago: University of Chicago Press, 1999.

Baldwin, *Pittsburgh, the Story of a City*. Pittsburg: University of Pittsburgh Press, 1937.

Birkbeck, Morris. *Letters from Illinois*. London: Taylor and Hessy, 1818.

Birkbeck, Morris. *Notes on a Journey in America, from the Coast of Virginia to the Territory of Illinois*. London: Ridgway and Sons, 1818.

Birkby, Evelyn Corrie. *Adventure After Sixty, Alone Through England and Scotland*. Sidney, Iowa: Honey Hill Books, 1985.

Birkby, Evelyn Corrie. *Our Corrie Family Records*. Sidney, Iowa: Honey Hill Books, 1994.

Birkby, Evelyn Corrie. "Up a Country Lane" newspaper columns. Shenandoah, Iowa: *The Shenandoah Evening Sentinel* and *The Valley News Today*, 1949-present.

Carmony, Donald. *Indiana 1816-1850; The Pioneer Era the history of Indiana, Vol. 11*. Indianapolis, Indiana: Indiana Historical Bureau and the Indiana Historical Society, 1998.

Corrie, Jessie. *The Records of the Corrie Family*. Jessie Corrie, 1899.

Corrie, James. *Our Corrie Family Records*. James Corrie.

Corrie, Miriam, transcriber. *Letters from an Old Desk*. Illinois State Historical Library.

Corrie, Timothy Jr. *Our Corrie Family Records 2001 Edition*, published 2001 by Tim's Basement Publishing, Redmond, WA.

Cory, Kathleen B. *Tracing Your Scottish Ancestry Second Edition*. Baltimore, Maryland: Genealogical Publishing Company, 1996.

Cramer, Zadok. *The Navigator, 1808*. Cincinnati, Ohio: Young and Klein, Inc., reprint, 1950.

Davis, James E. *Frontier Illinois*. Bloomington, Indiana: Indiana University Press, 1998.

Draffen, Thomas. *History of Terregles Church*. 1985.

Highways and Hedges: Fifty Years of Western Methodism. Custom printing. Portions saved by Wallace Beals in the Quintin Local History Center.

Ancestors. Iowa Public Television.

Krumm, Dallas, "Historically Yours," newspaper columns in the *Mt. Carmel Daily.* Albion, Illinois: Sumner Press and Prairie Post.

Lawrence County Historical Society. *Lawrence County, Illinois, Commemorative Edition, 175th Anniversary 1821-1996.* Paducah, Kentucky: Turner Publishing Company, 1996.

Least Heat-Moon, William. *River Horse, The Logbook of a Boat Across America.* New York: Houghton Mifflin Co, 1999.

McCluskey, Roy E. *You, Too, Root Out Your Roots.* Roy E. McCluskey, 1988.

Miller, Hamish. *Dowsing, A Journey Beyond Our Five Senses.* New York: Walker and Company, 2004.

Palmer, Joyce and Maurice. *A History of Wellingborough from Roman to Modern Times.* Northhampton, England, 1872.

Murray, M.M. and James M. Riddle. *The Pittsburgh Directory for 1819.* Pittsburgh: Butler & Lambdin, 1819.

Sanders, Scott Russell. *The Floating House.* New York: Aladdin Paperbacks, 1995.

Stephens, T. *Album of the Northhampshire Congregational Churches.* Wellingborough, England: Northants Printing and Publishing, 1894.

Thomas. "Peculiar River" from *Travels in America.* Riddle and Murray, 1806.

Thwaites, Reuben Gold. *Afloat on the Ohio: An Historical Pilgrimage of a Thousand Miles in a Skiff, from Redstone to Cairo.* Chicago: Way & Williams, 1897.

Wabash County Historical Society. *1824 History and Families-1993 Wabash County Illinois.* Marion, Kentucky: Riverbend Publishing Company, 1993.

Waud, A.R., *Harper's Weekly,* October 1867

World Book Encyclopedia. Chicago: Field Enterprise, 1957.

• • • • • • • • • • • • • • • • • • •

Unless otherwise noted, all photographs are from the collection of Evelyn Corrie Birkby.

Recipe Index

Genealogy Tips Index

About the Author

Evelyn Corrie Birkby is a wife, mother, homemaker, newspaper columnist, author, and radio personality who for over 50 years has enchanted her audience with her honest chatty ways, her warm stories, and wonderful recipes.

Photo by Mike Whye

Daughter of a Methodist minister, Evelyn lived most of her early years in small towns in Iowa. After college she taught school for four years and then worked as Director of Religious Education in the Grace United Methodist Church in Waterloo, Iowa. She later became Youth Director at the First United Methodist Church of Chicago. Evelyn married her high-school classmate Robert Birkby, and in 1948 they moved to a small farm south of Farragut, Iowa.

Since 1949, Evelyn has written a weekly column on rural Iowa life. The column, titled *Up a Country Lane*, was first written for the Shenandoah Evening Sentinel and currently for its successor, The Valley News Today. Since she started writing this column almost 60 years ago, Evelyn has the remarkable record of never having missed her weekly deadline.

Evelyn was also a "radio homemaker" for almost 40 years, broadcasting her warm words of wisdom on rural life over a five-state area on radio station KMA in Shenandoah, Iowa. For more than a quarter century Evelyn also was a regular monthly columnist for *Kitchen Klatter* magazine, and broadcast on the syndicated *Kitchen Klatter* radio program. Evelyn still airs a monthly radio visit with the KMA listening audience.

Evelyn is the author of ten books. Two of her most popular books are published by University of Iowa Press. *Neighboring on the Air* describes the heyday of radiohomemakers. *Up a Country Lane* stitches together stories, photographs and recipes from Iowa farm life in the 1940s and 1950s.

Among the publications that have reviewed Evelyn's books are the *Los Angeles Times*, the *New York Times*, the *Washington Post*, *Smithsonian Magazine*, *The Farm Journal*, *Successful Farming*, and many others. She has appeared on several national television programs, including the *Today Show* (CBS) and *Nightly News with Peter Jennings* (ABC). Evelyn was featured in a fifteen-page article in *New Yorker Magazine* in the early 1990s. Evelyn was also the inspiration for Neighbor Dorothy, the main character in three of novelist Fannie Flagg's popular books: *Welcome to the World Baby Girl, Standing in the Rainbow,* and *Can't Wait to Get to Heaven.*

Evelyn is the mother of three adventurous sons, one remarkable daughter-in-law, a "perfect" eleven-year-old grandson, and a delightful three-year-old granddaughter. Evelyn and her husband Robert live on picturesque Honey Hill in Sidney, Iowa.

Praise for author Evelyn Corrie Birkby

"Evelyn Birkby has discussed virtually everything of importance to her on the radio (and in her books). She has swapped recipes...she has delivered motivational talks when crops were bad, she has discussed training of children, the dressing of chickens and shared her tribulations as a wife and mother. Now she shares her passion for family history . . ."

—*New Yorker Magazine*, 1991
Michael & Jane Stern

"Birkby's journey drives home the point that every small town did not spawn well educated, neighborly homemakers who became media stars. Birkby writes of a sense of community and trust that is all too rare for residents of modern cities."

—Susanne Machnic
Los Angeles Times

"Residents in southwest Iowa feel they know Evelyn Birkby for her best-selling books Neighboring on the Air, and Up a Country Lane. She has a status that has extended throughout the US."

—*Simpsonian Magazine*

"Birkby's love and understanding of her subjects, her characters, even her recipes, reflect both the people and places in which she's been. Birkby's book is a lovingly written testimony of an important and unique part of history. Her books show a literary talent and a passion for rural history."

—Ed Haag
Farm Journal

"It is her tender-hearted scenes from the golden times past that so charm and move us now."

—*Midwest Today Magazine*

"I can remember my father's (Willard Archie) delight when he told the family that Evelyn had suggested writing a column for our newspaper. Our family and the Birkbys had many ties and he knew she would be an intelligent and genuine chronicler of rural life with an appeal well beyond her Fremont County neighborhood."

—David Archie,
Iowan Magazine

"Among Evelyn Birkby's many claims to fame--she's been a cookie judge at the Iowa State Fair for over 12 years. She's an author, too, It's a tribute to the power of Birkby's writing ability that the University of Iowa Press has published several books of her recipes, home talk, personal reminiscences and local history. It's also a tribute to Birkby's imagination that she can build word pictures and make you feel as if you have been to that place even if you've never been. You know what she is talking about."

—Paul Hendrickson in the *Washington Post*

Fannie Flagg toyed with several ideas for a few years before she decided she wasn't finished with autobiographical themes...In a small bookstore in Fair Hill, Alabama., Flagg spotted "Neighboring on the Air," She befriended the author, Evelyn Birkby of Sidney, Iowa, and with her help, Fannie began writing her next book . Her major character in "Standing in the Rainbow," based on Evelyn's radio homemakers, continued to appear in "Can't Wait to Get To Heaven."

—*Publisher's Weekly*

"The author takes a backward look straightforwardly! Though not sentimental, Birkby's is an affectionate record of living simply. It has a commonplace integrity that can seem, in our era, like fantasy."

—*Publishers Weekly*

"Evelyn has a way of writing that is so descriptive that you feel you are right there beside her wherever she's been and who she's talked to."

—Emily Bengtson--longtime friend and neighbor

Evelyn Birkby is a master storyteller and homemaker whose chatty newspaper columns and radio commentaries have entertained, comforted and educated Midwesterners for nearly 60 years. She's done it so well that The New Yorker magazine in 1991 did a 15-page feature on her, and she wound up on all the TV network news shows. This new book "Witching for William" may be Evelyn's best story ever, and certainly the deepest reporting job she's ever done. It is a search for, and profile of, her long-lost great-great-grandfather William Corrie. She turns it into a riveting adventure. What makes it so for general readers like us is not that Evelyn's family is so much more interesting than yours or mine, but that she tells the story so much better than most of us could. It's helpful that she includes genealogy tips at the end of each chapter. And it's perfect that she includes a fitting recipe after each chapter, too. Her first boss in the newspaper business told her in 1949 always to put a recipe at the end of every column she wrote "because they may not read anything else but they'll always read a recipe." That advice has served her – and her readers – very well, and the recipes in "Witching for William" make it possible for you not only to read this story but also to taste it.

—from Iowa writer Chuck Offenburger

Evelyn Birkby's Witching for William is many things: part genealogy, part how-to, part who-dun-it, part collection of historic recipes and part honest-to-God history. The reader starts off learning about an amiable woman's search for her ancestors with tips on how to do the same for one's own. After a while, she introduces them to us. Soon, they begin to speak for themselves and the times they lived in. In the end, Birkby achieves what Shelly said Shakespeare had, "negative capability"; she disappears, as storyteller, into the characters in the tale she is relating. In other words, the history she has so painstakingly researched comes alive. The greatest compliment one can give an historian is to say, "It was like she was there." It was like Evelyn Birkby was there and we were too through her excellent and spirited writing.

—Michael Carey, winner of the Iowa Library
Association's Brigham Plaque Award and the
Des Moines LibraryFoundation's Iowa Author Award.

Also by Evelyn Birkby

Festival Cookie Book

Come Again Cookie Book

Cooking With the KMA Radio Homemakers

Adventure After Sixty; Alone through England and Scotland

Neighboring on the Air Cookbook

Up a County Lane Cookbook

Our Corrie Family Records

The Birkby Family Heritage

History of the Sidney, Iowa United Methodist Church; 150 Years
of Blessings 1852-2002

Weekly newspaper columns for the *Shenandoah (Iowa) Evening
Sentinel* and *The Valley News Today* beginning in 1949 and continuing—

For more information, visit www.honeyhillbooks.com

HONEY HILL
B·O·O·K·S

Books by Evelyn Corrie Birkby

1. In 1983, Evelyn was asked by radio station KMA to develop a Book Department for the station. Her first project was to take the garbage bags filled with recipes from the station's annual Cookie Festivals and make them into a cook book. Since every person who came to those cookie teas was asked to bring a plate of cookies and the recipe that meant she had hundreds of good recipes from which to choose. The result was **"The Festival Cookie Book."** It was an instant success.

2. The first cookie book sold so well, and as more festivals were held and more recipes were acquired, KMA decided if one book was good than "come again" and get another. Thus **"The Come Again Cookie Book"** was born. Now Evelyn was experienced in the entire process of choosing the recipes, doing the layout of the pages, finding clever little pictures to include, shepherding it through the printing process, and marketing the book. Like the first cookie book, this one quickly became a best seller.

3. Evelyn had been a radio homemaker starting in 1950, so she personally was acquainted with the women broadcasters, several going back to the beginning of radio in the Midwest. She felt that these pioneers of early

radio were too important to be forgotten so her next book was **"Cooking with the KMA Radio Homemakers,"** It included the story of their lives, pictures of events and their favorite recipes. As she had done before, Evelyn saw this book through the layout and printing process and the marketing as well.

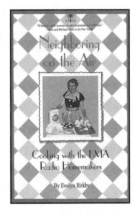

4. When the University of Iowa Press discovered the story of the radio homemakers they approached Evelyn and asked her if she would update the book, and add more stories, pictures and recipes. They published a new book, **"Neighboring on the Air Cookbook."** It became one of the University of Iowa Press' best sellers.

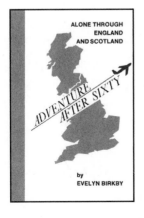

5. **"Adventure After Sixty"** started as newspaper columns. Publisher of the Shenandoah Evening Sentinel, Louise Tinley, wrote in the Foreword, "When I started reading (Evelyn's) columns about her trip to England and Scotland, I was so impressed I encouraged her to put the stories together and have them published as a book." A number of the stories from this book have now found their way into "Witching for William" since the trips Evelyn took to Britain included finding relatives and researching the places where Corries from the past had lived.

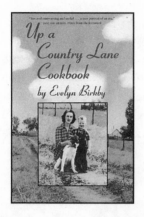

6. "Up A Country Lane" is the name given to Evelyn's long-running newspaper column. When she started putting a book by the same name together she expected it to be a series of her columns. But it did not work out as expected. After reworking the book several times, the finished manuscript became the story of life on a small Iowa farm in the 40s and 50s; a story of a way of life now all but gone. Evelyn tells how the Birkby family farmed, grew a garden, shared life in the community, and began their family. She added recipes, now an integral part of her writings, The University of Iowa Press published **"Up a Country Lane Cookbook"** and it became one of their best selling books.

7. It was natural for Evelyn to follow her interest in family history into the genealogy world. She learned the ups and down of research, how to identify and number relatives and found her best helper was the computer. In time for the Corrie family reunion, she published her findings in a book she called simply, **"The Corrie Family Records."** This book became a valuable resource for "Witching for William."

8. Not one to neglect her husband Robert's family, Evelyn researched the Birkby family and put together her second genealogy book. **"The Birkby**

Family Heritage." It came off the press just in time for a big Birkby family reunion on the southwest Iowa farm settled by Robert's great grandfather and still owned by a cousin, Jerry Birkby.

OUR BIRKBY
FAMILY
HERITAGE

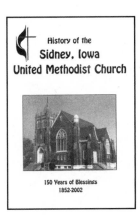

History of the
Sidney, Iowa
United Methodist Church

150 Years of Blessings
1852-2002

9. Most churches have interesting histories and the Sidney United Methodist church is no exception. When it had its 150th anniversary, it fell to Evelyn to put together its fascinating history. She wrote a book that can be helpful for any church that wishes to put together a similar record, for it includes the early circuit riders, how the local parish evolved, up through the life stories of the ministers who have served the congregation, including Evelyn's father, the Rev. Carl M. Corrie.

10. **"Witching for William"** really did start around the table in that little frame farmhouse in eastern Illinois when Evelyn's father, Carl Corrie first heard the stories of the family. It took many year for Evelyn to add information, visiting with relatives, and getting together in a great family re-union, for this book to materialize. Evelyn's hope is that those who read it will enjoy the journey and be inspired to start their own.

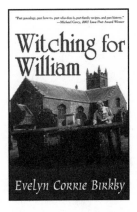

"Part genealogy, part how-to, part who-dun-it, part family recipes, and part history."
—Michael Carey, 2007 Iowa Poet Award Winner

Witching for
William

Evelyn Corrie Birkby